AWS LAMBA

A Hands-On, In-Depth Guide to Serverless Microservices

Jason Clothier

Disclaimer and Terms of Use

Table Of Contents

Chapter one: Introduction - What Is Serverless?

The term serverless grew in popularity as Amazon first launched AWS Lambda in 2014. Since then it has grown in both usage and reference, as more and more retailers enter the market with their own solutions.

Serverless Computing is a computing code execution model where the developers are relieved of several time-consuming activities so that they can focus on other important tasks. This trend is also known as Function as a Service (FaaS) where the cloud vendor is responsible for starting and stopping a function's container platform, check infrastructure security, reduce maintenance efforts, improve scalability, so on and so forth at low operational costs. The aim is to develop microservice oriented solutions to help decompose complex applications into small, easily manageable and exchangeable modules.

Ever heard of Serverless computing? If you haven't, you should know that it is the new hype word in IT. The term 'Serverless Computing' talks about an application of implementation where the server is abstracted away. This does not mean that there are no web servers, it's just that you don't have to supply the web servers by yourself. It's a modern way of internet hosting service programs and solutions on facilities which are not managed by the customers. In serverless processing, sources are provisioned on reasoning only when a specific occasion occurs. Resources are no longer allocated only to stay non-productive until called upon. In some cases, serverless infra can free your business from the running costs of maintaining infra, improvements, and provisioning web servers.

Time spent in establishing the reasoning facilities for scalability is also reduced as serverless processing guarantees faster distribution and extremely reliable programs. Serverless processing is an application of reasoning processing, but in this case, the Cloud Services Company controls the provisioning of sources on runtime foundation rather than preparing storage space potential in enhancing, and consumers just have to pay for what they use instead of buying prevents of storage space in enhance. It is much more granular, and thus more cost-effective as compared to the standard reasoning component. Applications may seem to be 'serverless' as server management, maintenance, as well as potential preparing, are completely invisible from the customers. The normalization of serverless processing is a major hop towards growing the capability to perform complex projects without the need of expensive elements. Manufacturers going from atlas Sian to fashion have made the jump to serverless determining, according to a presentation named 'The Condition of Serverless Computing' by Amazon Web Services.

Let's see what server less processing means on a technical level? It's a process where designers can set up solutions from little features, strikes are foundations of the rule. The little rule prevents can be accomplished in reaction to particular request call. These features are sometimes-infrequent app elements, activated when needed by factors. This data is held in a unique atmosphere that syncs with the active production atmosphere.

Why is Serverless processing essential as a paradigm?

Serverless processing is a progress of the little solutions approach to architecting programs and programs. The idea behind this is to let the Cloud Support Provider's handle the fundamental estimate infra and let designers focus only on the performance that needs to be provided. Here are some advantages:

- Ideal for event-driven scenarios: The conventional auto-scaling feature can have critical warm-up periods for groups and climb, both during up-scaling and down-scaling and it is also possible that it may not be an extension. Serverless is a perfect processing design when it comes to the performance of little prevents of rule aka features as they turn out to be the reaction to occasion activates and you pay only for the Fraxel resource periods that you actually absorbed. Thus, preserving a lot of expenses. Serverless processing is maximum for event-driven architectures, for example, the Internet of Things circumstances.

- Assemble low-cost little solutions architecture: By going serverless, a lot of reasoning processing features can be accomplished at once. These features are separate from each other in reaction to the occasion reflecting at once in the performance. The smaller prevents of the rule set up in serverless processing are simple to handle and the examining becomes simple too. The various features in the reasoning atmosphere can themselves reveal clean, Representational Condition Transfer (RESTful) connections to perform with more such features of an app. Application designers can quickly put together a structure reflecting little solutions by applying several reasoning features that perform together. Most leading system designers are applying this strategy to set up software in a cost-effective way.

Despite these benefits, there are some restrictions in the serverless atmosphere. A limitation on the size of the rule is found and which when implemented facilitates only a few development 'languages.' The typical rule prevents and monolithic, i.e., single-tiered software application architectures should also be ignored. Another limitation is that designers should be extremely regimented in the way they are using serverless processing.

Big savings with Server less infra

Serverless design helps cut on a lot of prices. About 60 percent price preserving is obtained along with considerably lower management initiatives. This computation is based on an e-Commerce app using Lambda by Amazon Web Services which is a Function as something design, compared to internet hosting service the app on Amazon Flexible Compute Cloud (EC2) by Amazon Web Support and instances in a high accessibility structure were measured on per hour basis foundation. Serverless processing is all set to rise as interest and adopting grow. Various tools to handle multiple kinds of features and substance service development are changing using serverless processing.

This brings us to the question - are there really 'serverless' computing services?

Of course, it is only logical that there should be servers in the background, but developers need not bother about the operation or provisioning of these servers; the entire server management is done by the cloud provider. Thus, the developer can devote more of his time to creating effective and innovative codes.

How does it work?

Being serverless, the developers are relieved from the tension of server operation and maintenance and hence can focus on the codes.

The developer gets access to a framework with which he can

create codes, which are adaptable for IoT applications as well, and that means handling the exodus of inputs and outputs. The cause and effect of the code will be reflected in the framework.

- It takes on the role of a service, by providing all requisites for a functioning application.
- The upsides and downsides of serverless computing
- Serverless computing has the following benefits:
- It Saves Time and Overhead Costs

Many large companies like Coca-Cola and The Seattle Times are already leveraging the benefits of serverless computing to help trigger code in response to a series of pre-defined events. This helps them to manage their fleet of servers without the threat of overhead costs.

One of the main attractions of serverless computing is that it is a 'pay as you use' model. You just need to pay for the runtime of your function - the duration your code is executed and the number of times it's been triggered. You don't have to incur the cost of unutilized functions as seen in a cloud computing model where even 'idle' resources must be paid for.

Nanoservices takes Serverless Computing to a Whole New Level

Serverless architecture gives you the chance to work with several architectures including nano-services. It is these architectures that help you structure your serverless computing application. You can say that Nanoservices is the first architectural pattern because of each functionality comes with its own API endpoint and its own separate function file.

Each of the API endpoints points to one function file that implements one CRUD (Create, Retrieve, Update, Delete) functionality. It works in perfect correlation with microservices, another architecture of serverless computing, and enables auto-scaling and load balancing. You no longer have to manually configure clusters and load balancers.

Enjoy an Event-based Compute Experience

Companies are always worried about infrastructure costs and provisioning of servers when their Functions call rate become very high. Serverless providers like Microsoft Azure are a perfect solution for situations like this as they aim to provide an event-based serverless compute experience to aid in faster app development.

It is event-driven, and developers no longer have to rely on the ops to test their code. They can quickly run, test and deploy their code without getting tangled in the traditional workflow.

Scaling as Per the Size of the Workload

Serverless Computing automatically scales your application. With each individual trigger, your code will run parallel to it, thereby reducing your workload and saving time in the process. When the code is not running, you don't have to pay anything.

The charging takes place for every 100ms your code executes and for the number of times the code is triggered. This is a good thing because you no longer pay for an idle computer.

Developers can Quit Worrying about the Machinery the Code Runs on

The promise given to developers through IaaS (Infrastructure as a Service)- one of the service models of cloud computing and serverless computing is that they can stop worrying about how many machines are needed at any given point of time, especially during peak hours, whether the machines are working optimally, whether all the security measures are offered and so on.

The software teams can forget about the hardware, concentrate on the task at hand and dramatically reduce costs. This is because they no longer have to worry about hardware capacity requirements nor make long-term server reservation contracts.

Downsides Of Serverless Computing

Performance issue.

Serverless computing cannot be considered the perfect approach due to performance issues. The model itself means that you obtain a higher latency in the way that the calculation sources respond to the requirements of the application. It would be better if you use dedicated virtual servers if performance is your primary requirement.

Debugging and monitoring serverless computing is also difficult. Because you use a single server source, the debugging and monitoring functions become extremely difficult. (In this respect, the good news is that the tools that manage debugging and monitoring will eventually arrive in the serverless environments)

You will be bound to your provider.

It's often hard to make changes in the platform or switch providers without making changes in application as well.

Serverless most often refers to serverless applications. Serverless applications are ones that don't require you to provision or manage any servers. You can focus on your core product and business logic instead of responsibilities like operating system (OS) access control, OS patching, provisioning, right-sizing, scaling, and availability. By building your application on a serverless platform, the platform manages these responsibilities for you.

For service or platform to be considered serverless, it should provide the following capabilities:

- No server management – You don't have to provide or maintain any servers. There are no software or runtime to install, maintain, or administer.
- Flexible scaling – You can range your program instantly or by modifying its capacity through toggling the models of consumption (for example, throughput, memory) rather than units of personal web servers.
- High availability – Serverless programs have built-in availability. You don't need to designer for these capabilities because the services running the application offer them by default.
- No nonproductive capacity – You don't have to pay for idle capacity. There is no need for pre-provision or over-provision capacity for factors like processing and storage space. There is no charge when your code isn't operating.

The AWS Cloud provides many different services that can be components of a serverless application. These include capabilities for:

- Compute – AWS Lambda
- APIs – Amazon API Gateway
- Storage – Amazon Simple Storage Service (Amazon S3)
- Databases –Amazon DynamoDB
- Interprocess messaging – Amazon Simple Notification Service (Amazon SNS) and Amazon Simple Queue Service (Amazon SQS)
- Orchestration – AWS Step Functions and Amazon CloudWatch Events
- Analytics – Amazon Kinesis

This whitepaper will focus on AWS Lambda, the compute layer of your serverless application where your code is executed, and the AWS developer tools and services that enable best practices when building and maintaining serverless applications with Lambda

What Is AWS Lambda?

AWS Lambda is a serverless computing service that operates your rule in reaction to activities and instantly controls the actual estimate sources for you. You can use AWS Lambda to increase other AWS solutions with custom reasoning or make your own back-end solutions that operate at AWS range, performance, and protection. AWS Lambda can instantly run rule in reaction to multiple activities, such as HTTP demands via Amazon.com API Entrance, variations to things in Amazon.com S3 pails, desk up-dates in Amazon.com DynamoDB, and state changes in AWS Step Features.

Lambda operates your rule on high-availability estimate facilities and works all the administration of the estimate sources, such as server and OS maintenance, capacity provisioning and automatic climbing, rule, and protection spot implementation, and rule tracking and signing. All you need to do is supply the rule.

Introducing AWS Lambda functions

The rule you run on AWS Lambda is called a "Lambda operate." After you make your Lambda operate it is always ready to run as soon as it is activated, similar to a formula in a worksheet. Each operates includes your rule as well as some associated settings information, such as the operating name and source requirements. Lambda functions are "stateless," with no appreciation to the actual facilities so that Lambda can rapidly launch as many duplicates of the operation as required to the range to the rate of inbound activities.

After you publish your rule to AWS Lambda, you can associate your operate with specific AWS sources (e.g., a particular Amazon.com S3 pail, Amazon.com DynamoDB desk, Amazon.com Kinesis stream, or Amazon.com SNS notification). Then, when the source changes, Lambda will execute your operate and manage the estimate sources as required in order to keep up with inbound demands.

When Should I Use AWS Lambda Function?

AWS Lambda is a perfect computing platform for many application scenarios, provided that you can write your application rule in languages supported by AWS Lambda (that is, Node.js, Java, Go and C# and Python), and run within the AWS Lambda standard runtime environment and sources provided by Lambda.

AWS Lambda to execute operational and administrative actions on your behalf, including provisioning capacity, tracking fleet wellness, applying security patches, deploying your code, and monitoring and logging your Lambda functions.

If you need to manage your own processing resources, Amazon Web Services also provides other computer solutions to meet your needs.

- Amazon Elastic Compute Reasoning (Amazon EC2) support provides flexibility and a wide range of EC2 example types to choose from. It gives you the option to customize operating techniques, network and security settings, and the entire application stack, but you are accountable for provisioning capacity, tracking fleet health and efficiency, and using Availability Areas for mistake patience.

- Elastic Beanstalk offers an easy-to-use service for deploying and scaling programs onto Amazon EC2 in which you retain ownership and complete control over the underlying EC2 circumstances.

Lambda is a high-scale, provision-free serverless compute offering based on functions. It provides the cloud logic layer for your application. Lambda functions can be triggered by a variety of events that occur on AWS or on supporting third-party services. They enable you to build reactive, event-driven systems. When there are multiple, simultaneous events to respond to, Lambda simply runs more copies of the function in parallel. Lambda functions scale precisely with the size of the workload, down to the individual request. Thus, the likelihood of having an idle server or container is extremely low. Architectures that use Lambda functions are designed to reduce wasted capacity. Lambda can be described as a type of serverless Function-as-a-Service (FaaS).

FaaS is one approach to building event-driven computing systems. It relies on functions as the unit of deployment and execution. Serverless FaaS is a type of FaaS where no virtual machines or containers are present in the programming model and where the vendor provides provision-free scalability and built-in reliability.

Figure 1 shows the relationship among event-driven computing, FaaS, and serverless FaaS.

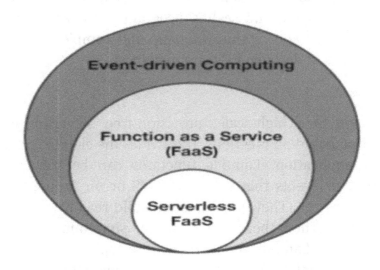

Figure 1: The relationship among event-driven computing, Faas and serverless Faas

With Lambda, you can run code for virtually any type of application or backend service. Lambda runs and scales your code with high availability.

An example event source is API Gateway, which can invoke a Lambda function anytime an API method created with API Gateway receives an HTTPS request. Another example is Amazon SNS, which has the ability to invoke a Lambda function anytime a new message is posted to an SNS topic.

You don't need to write any code to integrate an event source with your Lambda function, manage any of the infrastructures that detects events and delivers them to your function, or manage to scale your Lambda function to match the number of events that are delivered. You can focus on your application logic and configure the event sources that cause your logic to run.

Your Lambda function runs within a (simplified) architecture that looks like the one shown in Figure 2

Figure 2. simplified architecture of a running Lambda function

Lambda Function Code

At its core, you use Lambda to execute code. This can be code that you've written in any of the languages supported by Lambda (Java, Node.js, Python, or C# as of this publication), as well as any code or packages you've uploaded alongside the code that you've written. You're free to bring any libraries, artifacts, or compiled native binaries that can execute on top of the runtime environment as part of your function code package. If you want, you can even execute code you've written in another programming language (PHP, Go, SmallTalk, Ruby, etc.), as long as you stage and invoke that code from within one of the support languages in the AWS Lambda runtime environment.

The Lambda runtime environment is based on an Amazon Linux AMI, so you should compile and test the components you plan to run inside of Lambda within a matching environment. To help you perform this type of testing prior to running within Lambda, AWS provides a set of tools called AWS SAM Local to enable local testing of Lambda functions. We discuss these tools in the Serverless Development Best Practices section of this whitepaper.

The Function Code Package

The function code package contains all of the assets you want to have available locally upon execution of your code. A package will, at minimum, include the code function you want the Lambda service to execute when your function is invoked. However, it might also contain other assets that your code will reference upon execution, for example, additional files, classes, and libraries that your code will import, binaries that you would like to execute, or configuration files that your code might reference upon invocation. The maximum size of a function code package is 50 MB compressed and 250MB extracted at the time of this publication.

When you create a Lambda function (through the AWS Management Console, or using the CreateFunction API) you can reference the S3 bucket and object key where you've uploaded the package. Alternatively, you can upload the code package directly when you create the function. Lambda will then store your code package in an S3 bucket managed by the service. The same options are available when you publish updated code to existing Lambda functions.

As events occur, your code package will be downloaded from the S3 bucket, installed in the Lambda runtime environment, and invoked as needed. This happens on demand, at the scale required by the number of events triggering your function, within an environment managed by Lambda.

The Handler

When a Lambda function is invoked, code execution begins at what is called the handler. The handler is a specific code method (Java, C#) or function (Node.js, Python) that you've created and included in your package. You specify the handler when creating a Lambda function. Each language supported by

Lambda has its own requirements for how a function handler can be defined and referenced within the package.

Once the handler is successfully invoked inside your Lambda function, the runtime environment belongs to the code you've written. Your Lambda function is free to execute any logic you see fit, driven by the code you've written that starts in the handler. gateway response means your handler can call other methods and functions within the files and classes you've uploaded. Your code can import third-party libraries that you've uploaded, and install and execute native binaries that you've uploaded (as long as they can run on Amazon Linux). It can also interact with other AWS services or make API requests to web services that it depends on, etc.

The Event Object

When your Lambda function cloud formation in one of the supported languages, one of the parameters provided to your handler function is an event object. The event differs in structure and contents, depending on which event source created it. The contents of the event parameter include all of the data and metadata your Lambda function needs to drive its logic. For example, an event created by API Gateway will contain details related to the HTTPS request that was made by the API client (for example, path, query string, request body), whereas an event created by Amazon S3 when a new object is created will include details about the bucket and the new object.

The Context Object

Your Lambda function is also provided with a context object. The context object allows your function code to interact with the Lambda execution environment. The contents and structure of the context object vary, based on the language

25

runtime your Lambda function is using, but at minimum, it will contain:

- AWS RequestId – Used to track specific invocations of a Lambda function (important for error reporting or when contacting AWS Support).
- Remaining time – The amount of time in milliseconds that remain before your function timeout occurs (Lambda functions can run a maximum of 300 seconds as of this publishing, but you can configure a shorter timeout).
- Logging – Each language runtime provides the ability to stream log statements to Amazon CloudWatch Logs. The context object contains information about which CloudWatch Logs stream your log statements will be sent to. For more information about how logging is handled in each language runtime, see the following:
  - Java24
  - Node.js25
  - Python26
  - C#27

Writing Code for AWS Lambda—Statelessness and Reuse

It's important to understand the central tenant when writing code for Lambda: your code cannot make assumptions about state. This is because Lambda fully manages when a new function container will be created and invoked for the first time. A container could be getting invoked for the first time for a number of reasons. For example, the events triggering your Lambda function are increasing in concurrency beyond the number of containers previously created for your function, an event is triggering your Lambda function for the first time in several minutes, etc. While Lambda is responsible for scaling your function containers up and down to meet actual demand, your code needs to be able to operate accordingly. Although Lambda won't interrupt the processing of a specific invocation that's already in flight, your code doesn't need to account for that level of volatility.

This means that your code cannot make any assumptions that state will be preserved from one invocation to the next. However, each time a function container is created and invoked, it remains active and available for subsequent invocations for at least a few minutes before it is terminated. When subsequent invocations occur on a container that has already been active and invoked at least once before, we say that invocation is running on a warm container.

When an invocation occurs for a Lambda function that requires your function code package to be created and invoked for the first time, we say the invocation is experiencing a cold start.

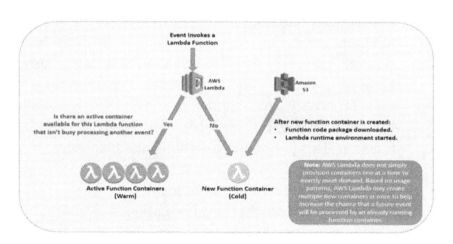

Figure 3. Invocations of warm function containers and cold function containers

Lambda Function Event Sources

Now that you know what goes into the code of a Lambda function, let's look at the event sources, or triggers, that invoke your code. While Lambda provides the Invoke API that enables you to directly invoke your function, you will likely only use it for testing and operational purposes.29 Instead, you can associate your Lambda function with event sources occurring within AWS services that will invoke your function as needed. You don't have to write, scale, or maintain any of the software that integrates the event source with your Lambda function.

Invocation Patterns

There are two models for invoking a Lambda function:

- Push Model – Your Lambda function is invoked every time a particular event occurs within another AWS service (for example, a new object is added to an S3 bucket).
- Pull Model – Lambda polls a data source and invokes your function with any new records that arrive at the data source, batching new records together in a single function invocation (for example, new records in an Amazon Kinesis or Amazon DynamoDB stream). Also, a Lambda function can be executed synchronously or asynchronously. You choose this using the parameter InvocationType HTTP when invoking a Lambda function. This parameter has three possible values:
- RequestResponse – Execute synchronously.
- Event – Execute asynchronously.
- DryRun – Test that the invocation is permitted for the caller, but don't execute the function.

Each event source dictates how your function can be invoked. The event source is also responsible for crafting its own event parameter, as we discussed earlier.

Lambda Function Configuration

After you write and package your Lambda function code, on top of choosing which event sources will trigger your function, you have various configuration options to set that defines how your code is executed within Lambda.

Function Memory

To define the resources allocated to your executing Lambda function, you're provided with a single dial to increase/decrease function resources:

Memory/RAM. You can allocate 128 MB of RAM up to 1.5 GB of RAM to your Lambda function. Not only will this dictate the amount of memory available to your function code during execution, but the same dial will also influence the CPU and network resources available to your function.

Selecting the appropriate memory allocation is a very important step when optimizing the price and performance of any Lambda function. Please review the best practices later in this whitepaper for more specifics on optimizing performance.

Versions and Aliases

There are times where you might need to reference or revert your Lambda function back to code that was previously deployed. Lambda lets you version your AWS Lambda functions. Each and every Lambda function has a default version built in: $LATEST. You can address the most recent code that has been uploaded to your Lambda function through the $LATEST version. You can take a snapshot of the code that's currently referred to by $LATEST and create a numbered version through the PublishVersion API. Also, when updating your function code through the UpdateFunctionCode API, there is an optional Boolean parameter, publish. By setting publish: true in your request, Lambda will create a new Lambda function version, incremented from the last published version.

You can invoke each version of your Lambda function independently, at any time. Each version has its own Amazon Resource Name (ARN), referenced like this:

arn:aws:lambda:[region]:[account]:function:[fn_name]:[version]

When calling the Invoke API or creating an event source for your Lambda function, you can also specify a specific version of the Lambda function to be executed. If you don't provide a version number, or use the ARN that doesn't contain the version number, $LATEST is invoked by default.

It's important to know that a Lambda function container is specific to a particular version of your function. So, for example, if there are already several function containers deployed and available in the Lambda runtime environment for version 5 of the function, version 6 of the same function will not be able to execute on top of the existing version 5 containers—a different set of containers will be installed and managed for each function version.

Invoking your Lambda functions by their version numbers can be useful during testing and operational activities. However, we don't recommend having your Lambda function be triggered by a specific version number for real application traffic. Doing so would require you to update all of the triggers and clients invoking your Lambda function to point at a new function version each time you wanted to update your code. Lambda aliases should be used here, instead. A function alias allows you to invoke and point event sources to a specific Lambda function version.

However, you can update what version that alias refers to at any time. For example, your event sources and clients that are invoking version number 5 through the alias live may cut over to version number 6 of your function as soon as you update the live alias to instead point at version number 6. Each alias can be referred to within the ARN, similar to when referring to a function version number:

arn:aws:lambda:[region]:[account]:function:[fn_name]:[alias]

Note: An alias is simply a pointer to a specific version number. This means that if you have multiple different aliases pointed to the same Lambda function version at once, requests to each alias are executed on top of the same set of installed function containers. This is important to understand so that you don't mistakenly point multiple aliases at the same function version number if requests for each alias are intended to be processed separately.

Here are some example suggestions for Lambda aliases and how you might use them:

- live/prod/active – This could represent the Lambda function version that your production triggers or that clients are integrating with.
- blue/green – Enable the blue/green deployment pattern through the use of aliases.
- debug – If you've created a testing stack to debug your applications, it can integrate with an alias like this when you need to perform a deeper analysis.

Creating a good, documented strategy for your use of function aliases enables you to have sophisticated serverless deployment and operations practices.

IAM Role

AWS Identity and Access Management (IAM) provides the capability to create IAM policies that define permissions for interacting with AWS services and APIs. Policies can be associated with IAM roles. Any access key ID and secret access key generated for a particular role is authorized to perform the actions defined in the policies attached to that role. In the context of Lambda, you assign an IAM role (called an execution role) to each of your Lambda functions. The IAM policies attached to that role define what AWS service APIs your function code is authorized to interact with. There are two benefits:

- Your source code isn't required to perform any AWS credential management or rotation to interact with the AWS APIs. Simply using the AWS SDKs and the default credential provider results in your Lambda function automatically using temporary credentials associated with the execution role assigned to the function.
- Your source code is decoupled from its own security posture. If a developer attempts to change your Lambda function code to integrate with a service that the function doesn't have access to, that integration will fail due to the IAM role assigned to your function. (Unless they have used IAM credentials that are separate from the execution role, you should use static code analysis tools to ensure that no AWS credentials are present in your source code).

It's important to assign each of your Lambda functions a specific, separate, and least-privilege IAM role. This strategy ensures that each Lambda function can evolve independently without increasing the authorization scope of any other Lambda functions.

Lambda Function Permissions

You can define which push model event sources are allowed to invoke a Lambda function through a concept called permissions. With permissions, you declare a functioning policy that lists the AWS Resource Names (ARNs) that are allowed to invoke a function. For pull model event sources (for example, Kinesis streams and DynamoDB streams), you need to ensure that the appropriate actions are permitted by the IAM execution role assigned to your Lambda function. AWS provides a set of managed IAM roles associated with each of the pull-based event sources if you don't want to manage thepermissions required. However, to ensure least privilege IAM policies, you should create your own IAM roles with resource-specific policies to permit access to just the intended event source.

Network Configuration

Executing your Lambda function occurs through the use of the Invoke API that is part of the AWS Lambda service APIs; so, there is no direct inbound network access to your function to manage. However, your function code might need to integrate with external dependencies (internal or publically hosted web services, AWS services, databases, etc.). A Lambda function has two broad options for outbound network connectivity:

- Default – Your Lambda function communicates from inside a virtual private cloud (VPC) that is managed by Lambda. It can connect to the internet, but not to any privately deployed resources running within your own VPCs.
- VPC – Your Lambda function communicates through an Elastic Network Interface (ENI) that is provisioned within the VPC and subnets you choose within your own account. These ENIs can be assigned security groups,

and traffic will route based on the route tables of the subnets those ENIs are placed within—just the same as if an EC2 instance were placed in the same subnet.

If your Lambda function doesn't require connectivity to any privately deployed resources, we recommend you select the default networking option. Choosing the VPC option will require you to manage:

- Selecting appropriate subnets to ensure multiple Availability Zones are being used for the purposes of high availability.
- Allocating the appropriate number of IP addresses to each subnet to manage capacity.
- Implementing a VPC network design that will permit your Lambda functions to have the connectivity and security required.

An increase in Lambda cold start times if your Lambda function invocation patterns require a new ENI to be created just in time. (ENI creation can take many seconds today.) However, if your use case requires private connectivity, use the VPC option with Lambda.

Environment Variables

Software Development Life Cycle (SDLC) best practice dictates that developers separate their code and their config. You can achieve this by using environment variables with Lambda. Without making any changes to your code the environment variables for Lambda functions enables you to pass data to your function code and libraries majestically. By default, these variables are encrypted at rest. For any sensitive information that will be stored as a Lambda function environment variable, we recommend you encrypt those values using the AWS Key Management Service (AWS KMS) prior to function creation, storing the encrypted cyphertext as the variable value. Then have your Lambda function decrypt that variable in memory at execution time. Here are some examples of how you might decide to use environment variables:

- Log settings (FATAL, ERROR, INFO, DEBUG, etc.)
- Dependency and/or database connection strings and credentials
- Feature flags and toggles

Each version of your Lambda function can have its own environment variable values. However, once the values are established for a numbered Lambda function version, they cannot be changed. To make changes to your Lambda function environment variables, you can change them to the $LATEST version and then publish a new version that contains the new environment variable values. This enables you to always keep track of which environment variable values are associated with a previous version of your function. This is often important during a rollback procedure or when triaging the past state of an application.

Dead Letter Queues

Even in the serverless world, exceptions can still occur. (For example, perhaps you've uploaded new function code that doesn't allow the Lambda event to be parsed successfully, or there is an operational event within AWS that is preventing the function from being invoked.) For asynchronous event sources (the event InvocationType), AWS owns the client software that is responsible for invoking your function. AWS does not have the ability to synchronously notify you if the invocations are successful or not as invocations occur. If an exception occurs when trying to invoke your function in these models, the invocation will be attempted two more times (with back-off between the retries).

After the third attempt, the event is either discarded or placed onto a dead letter queue, if you configured one for the function.

A dead letter queue is either an SNS topic or SQS queue that you have designated as the destination for all failed invocation events. If a failure event occurs, the use of a dead letter queue allows you to retain just the messages that failed to be processed during the event. Once your function is able to be invoked again, you can target those failed events in the dead letter queue for reprocessing.

Timeout

You can designate the maximum amount of time a single function execution is allowed to complete before a timeout is returned. The maximum timeout for a Lambda function is 300 seconds at the time of this publication, which means a single invocation of a Lambda function cannot execute longer than 300 seconds.

You should not always set the timeout for a Lambda function to the maximum.

There are many cases where an application should fail fast. Because your Lambda function is billed based on execution time in 100-ms increments, avoiding lengthy timeouts for functions can prevent you from being billed while a function is simply waiting to timeout (perhaps an external dependency is unavailable, you've accidentally programmed an infinite loop or another similar scenario).

Also, once execution completes or a timeout occurs for your Lambda function and a response is returned, all execution ceases. This includes any background processes, subprocesses, or asynchronous processes that your Lambda function might have spawned during execution. So you should not rely on background or asynchronous processes for critical activities.

Your code should ensure those activities are completed prior to timeout or returning a response from your function.

Serverless Best Practices

Now that we've covered the components of a Lambda-based serverless application, let's cover some recommended best practices. There are many SDLC and server-based architecture best practices that are also true for serverless architectures: eliminate single points of failure, test changes prior to deployment, encrypt sensitive data, etc.

Designing and implementing security into your applications should always be priority number one—this doesn't change with a serverless architecture. The major difference for securing a serverless application compared to a server hosted application is obvious—there is no server for you to secure. However, you still need to think about your application's security. There is still a shared responsibility model for serverless security. With Lambda and serverless architectures, rather than implementing application security through things like antivirus/malware software, file integrity monitoring, intrusion detection/prevention systems, firewalls, etc., you ensure security best practices through writing secure application code, tight access control over source code changes, and following AWS security best practices for each of the services that your Lambda functions integrate with.

The following is a brief list of serverless security best practices that should apply to many serverless use cases, although your own specific security and compliance requirements should be well understood and might include more than we describe here.

a) One IAM Role per Function

Each and every Lambda function within your AWS account should have a 1:1 relationship with an IAM role. Even if multiple functions begin with exactly the same policy, always decouple your IAM roles so that you can ensure least privilege policies for the future of your function. For example, if you shared the IAM role of a Lambda function that needed access to an AWS KMS key across multiple Lambda functions, then all of those functions would now have access to the same encryption key.

b) Temporary AWS Credentials

You should not have any long-lived AWS credentials included within your Lambda function code or configuration. (This is a great use for static code analysis tools to ensure it never occurs in your code base!)

For most cases, the IAM execution role is all that's required to integrate with other AWS services. Simply create AWS service clients within your code through the AWS SDK without providing any credentials.

Reliability Best Practices

Serverless applications can be built to support mission-critical use cases. Just as with any mission-critical application, it's important that you architect with the mindset that Werner Vogels, CTO, Amazon.com, advocates for, "Everything fails all the time." For serverless applications, this could mean introducing logic bugs into your code, failing application dependencies, and other similar application-level issues that you should try and prevent and account for using existing best practices that will still apply to your serverless applications. For infrastructure-level service events, where you have abstracted away from the event for serverless applications, you should understand how you have architected your application to achieve high availability and fault tolerance.

High Availability

High-availability is important for production applications. The availability posture of your Lambda function depends on the number of Availability Zones it can be executed in. If your function uses the default network environment, it is automatically available to execute within all of the Availability Zones in that AWS Region. Nothing else is required to configure high availability for your function in the default network environment. If your function is deployed within your own VPC, the subnets (and their respective Availability Zones) define if your function remains available in the event of an Availability Zone outage.

Therefore, it's important that your VPC design includes subnets in multiple Availability Zones. In the event that an Availability Zone outage occurs, it's important that your remaining subnets continue to have adequate IP addresses to support the number of concurrent functions required.

Fault Tolerance

If the application availability you need requires you to take advantage of multiple AWS Regions, you must take this into account upfront in your design.

It's not a complex exercise to replicate your Lambda function code packages to multiple AWS Regions. What can be complex, like most multi-region application designs, is coordinating a failover decision across all tiers of your application stack? This means you need to understand and orchestrate the shift to another AWS Region—not just for your Lambda functions but also for you event sources (and dependencies further upstream of your event sources) and persistence layers. In the end, a multi-region architecture is very application specific.

The most important thing to do to make a multi-region design feasible is to account for it in your design up front.

Recovery

Consider how your serverless application should behave in the event that your functions cannot be executed. For use cases where API Gateway is used as the event source, this can be as simple as gracefully handling error messages and providing a viable, if degraded, user experience until your functions can be successfully executed again.

For asynchronous use cases, it can be very important to still ensure that no function invocations are lost during the outage period. To ensure that all received events are processed after your function has recovered, you should take advantage of dead letter queues and implement how to process events placed on that queue after recovery occurs.

Performance Efficiency Best Practices

Before we dive into performance best practices, keep in mind that if your use case can be achieved asynchronously, you might not need to be concerned with the performance of your function (other than to optimize costs). You can leverage one of the event sources that will use the event InvocationType or use the pull-based invocation model. Those methods alone might allow your application logic to proceed while Lambda continues to process the event separately. If Lambda function execution time is something you want to optimize, the execution duration of your Lambda function will be primarily impacted by three things (in order of simplest to optimize): the resources you allocate in the function configuration, the language runtime you choose, and the code you write.

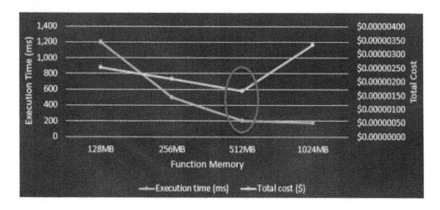

Figure 4. Choosing an optimal Lambda function memory size

Choosing the Optimal Memory Size

Lambda provides a single dial to turn up and down the amount of computing resources available to your function—the amount of RAM allocated to your function. The amount of allocated RAM also impacts the amount of CPU time and network bandwidth your function receives. Simply choosing the smallest resource amount that runs your function adequately fast is an anti-pattern. Because Lambda is billed in 100-ms increments, this strategy might not only add latency to your application, it might even be more expensive overall if the added latency outweighs the resource cost savings.

We recommend that you test your Lambda function at each of the available resource levels to determine what the optimal level of price/performance is for your application. You'll discover that the performance of your function should improve logarithmically as resource levels are increased. The logic you're executing will define the lower bound for function execution time. There will also be a resource threshold where any additional RAM/CPU/bandwidth available to your function no longer provides any substantial performance gain.

However, pricing increases linearly as the resource levels increase in Lambda. Your tests should find where the logarithmic function bends to choose the optimal configuration for your function.

The following graph shows how the ideal memory allocation to an example function can allow for both better cost and lower latency. Here, the additional compute cost per 100 ms for using 512 MB over the lower memory options is outweighed by the amount of latency reduced in the function by allocating more resources. But after 512 MB, the performance gains are diminished for this particular function's logic, so the additional cost per 100 ms now drives the total cost higher. This leaves 512 MB as the optimal choice for minimizing total cost.

Language Runtime Performance

Choosing a language runtime performance is obviously dependent on your level of comfort and skills with each of the supported runtimes. But if performance is the driving consideration for your application, the performance characteristics of each language are what you might expect on Lambda as you would in another runtime environment: the compiled languages (Java and .NET) incur the largest initial startup cost for a container's first invocation, but show the best performance for subsequent invocations. The interpreted languages (Node.js and Python) have very fast initial invocation times compared to the compiled languages, but can't reach the same level of maximum performance as the compiled languages do.

If your application use case is both very latency-sensitive and susceptible to incurring the initial invocation cost frequently (very spiky traffic or very infrequent use), we recommend one of the interpreted languages.

If your application does not experience large peaks or valleys within its traffic patterns or does not have user experiences blocked on Lambda function response times, we recommend you choose the language you're already most comfortable with.

Optimizing Your Code

Much of the performance of your Lambda function is dictated by what logic you need your Lambda function to execute and what its dependencies are. We won't cover what all those optimizations could be because they vary from application to application. But there are some general best practices to optimize your code for Lambda. These are related to taking advantage of container reuse (as describes in the previous overview) and minimizing the initial cost of a cold start.

Here are a few examples of how you can improve the performance of your function code when a warm container is invoked:

- After initial execution, store and reference any externalized configuration or dependencies that your code retrieves locally.
- Limit the reinitialization of variables/objects on every invocation (use global/static variables, singletons, etc.).
- Keep alive and reuse connections (HTTP, database, etc.) that were established during a previous invocation.

Finally, you should do the following to limit the amount of time that a cold start takes for your Lambda function:

1. Always use the default network environment unless connectivity to a resource within a VPC via private IP is required. This is because there are additional cold start scenarios related to the VPC configuration of a Lambda function (related to creating ENIs within your VPC).

2. Choose an interpreted language over a compiled language.
3. Trim your function code package to only its runtime necessities. This reduces the amount of time that it takes for your code package to be downloaded from Amazon S3 ahead of invocation.

Chapter Two: Serverless Microservices With AWS

In this chapter talks about how microservices, fly in the cloud, and serverless is just the next logical step. See serverless microservices in action using AWS.

What is serverless computing?

Serverless processing allows you to develop and run programs and services without considering about web servers. Serverless programs will not require that you supply, range, and handle any web servers. You can take shape them for nearly any type of program or after sales service, and everything needed to run and range your program with high accessibility is managed for you.

Why use serverless computing?

Building serverless programs means that your designers can concentrate on their primary product instead of concerning handling and working web servers or runtimes, either in the reasoning or on-premises. This decreased expense allows designers recover power and time that can be invested in creating great products which range and that are efficient.

What are the advantages of Serverless Microservices?

Focus on the rule, not servers

In monolithic programs, the designer has to keep the idea of the server because at all times. The characteristics of using an included microservice allow for various features to be run in similar without having affected efficiency. So long as each microservice is published to be computationally effective, a designer doesn't need to target the web servers.

Write the rule once, use it anywhere

Imagine operating at a large information company, and having the continuous problem of picture resizing across many of web qualities. A resizing microservice would allow any professional in the org to add the resizing plan the rule they're focusing on with a simple API call.

Language agnostic

Data Researchers often perform in Python or R, while the system group may be in Scala or Coffee. Because microservices connect via API it reveals up the chances for interoperability. Various open-source and cloud-based solutions are growing to improve the DevOps, popularly known as Be a Support or FaaS.

Composable

Microservices can simply be used together, like components in a formula, to get the result you're looking for. For example, you could have one microservice that holds all of the images on your site, operates each through a face identification microservice and a certificate dish identification microservice, delivers the images that contain encounters through something that blurs out each face, then delivers that picture back to your databases to exchange the uncensored picture. Over time, your company will develop up a profile of preferred microservices that can readily be found and consisting.

Cloud-agnostic

Microservices can give you the opportunity to use different blends of reasoning solutions. You may want to run your

AI/ML designs on one provider's high-performance GPUs while using a different company for cost-efficient databases internet hosting service.

Launch step-by-step features

Developers and groups can operate individually to create, set up, and range their microservices — they can also force repairs for insects without having affected all of the facilities. This significantly makes easier the orchestration of timeframes by Product and Dev Supervisors.

Compliments other reasoning services

Modern programs make a wide range of reasoning facilities that are on the market. Since these solutions are usually incorporated via APIs, microservices fit right in.

The financial aspects perform well

Serverless microservices are only unique up when needed and all of the most important hosts only cost for what you use (often by the second or 100ms intervals). The benefits can be large — especially for AI/ML designs that often have great estimate needs that come in jolts.

How a microservice works

There are several choices that you'll have to personalize to best fit your needs, but every microservice stocks some commonalities:

Your code

Your code is stateless and can get details via API, run the rule in the terminology of your choosing, and return its outcomes back again via API.

Your facilities Your facilities REALLY problems when it comes to microservices. There are serverless internet hosting support choices which manage protection, permissioning, GPU/CPU control, containerizing, terminology assistance, etc. There's a lot to think about, and if you don't wish to be doing a lot of large DevOps, we suggest using a handled program.

Your API endpoints This is how your microservice can get details in, and will deliver details out. If you need a refresher on APIs.

Your discoverability/versioning

You're going to need to develop some facilities that allow your group to edition APIs, monitor of who's accountable for what, and that can catalog the various microservices.

Challenges for Microservices

The details limitations of your company can be shown in your applications—services are distributed out so you'll need to use resources for finding, versioning, and interaction around each microservice. These resources are available but need either developing your own program or with a program designed for this.

You'll need to have obvious interaction on who's accountable for each microservice.

Testing and implementation can be more complicated, but resources are growing to improve these problems.

Microservice latencies are usually in milliseconds, but that's still a bit more slowly than phone calls within a monolithic support procedure. You'll obtain advantages by being able to run many microservices elastically in parallel—so the efficiency advantages over-shadow the expenses in applications of much complexness.

Create a Simple Lambda Function and Explore the Console

In this section, we will be giving the steps to create a simple Lambda function

To create a Lambda function

Sign in to the AWS Control System and open the AWS Lambda console.

Note that AWS Lambda provides a simple Hello World operate upon release under the How it works brand and contains a Run choice, providing you to produce the be a standard release. This guide presents additional choices you have to make, make sure enhance your Lambda functions, as well as other functions offered by the Lambda console and provides hyperlinks to each, welcoming you to understand more about each one in detail.

Choose to Make the purpose under the Get Began area to continue.

Note that the console reveals the Get Started page only if you do not have any Lambda functions designed. If you are creating functions already, you will see the Lambda > Functions page. On the list web page, select Make the purpose to go to the Create operate web page.

On the Create function page, you are offered with three options:

1. Author from scratch
2. Blueprints
3. Serverless Program Repository

If you'd like to evaluate the designs, select the Blueprints key, which will show the available designs. You can also use the Narrow to find for particular designs. For example:

49

Enter S3 in Narrow to get only the record of designs available to procedure Amazon.com S3 activities.

Enter dynamodb in Narrow to get a record of available designs to procedure Amazon.com DynamoDB activities.

For this Getting, Began work out, select the Writer from the beginning key.

In Author from the beginning, do the following:

- In Name*, specify your Lambda operate name.
- In Runtime*, select Python 3.6.
- In Role*, select Make a new part from the template(s):
- In Role name*, get into a name for your part.

Leave the Plan layouts area empty. For the reasons of this release, your Lambda operate will have the necessary performance authorizations.

Note that for an in-depth look at AWS Lambda's protection plans, see Verification and Accessibility Management for AWS Lambda.

Choose Make Function.

Under your new function-name page, observe the following:

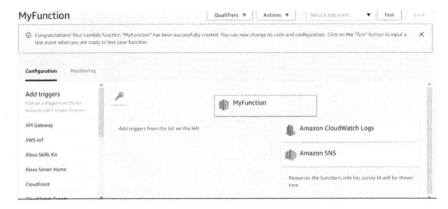

In the Add activates board, you can additionally select a support that instantly activates your Lambda operate by selecting one of the support choices detailed.

Depending on which support you select, you are persuaded to give appropriate information for that support. For example, if you select DynamoDB, you need to give the following:

- The name of the DynamoDB table
- Batch size
- Starting position
- For this example, do not set up an induce.
- Function rule, remember that rule is offered. It profits a simple "Hello from Lambda" introduction.
- Handler reveals lambda_function.lambda_handler value. It is the filename.handler-function. The system helps you to save the example rule in the lambda_function.py computer file and in the rule lambda_handler is the operate name that gets the occasion as a parameter when the Lambda operate is invoked

Other settings options on this page include:

Environment factors:

Environment factors for Lambda features allow you to dynamically pass configurations to your operate rule and collections, without making changes to your rule. For more details,

Tags:

Tags are key-value sets that you connect to AWS resources to better get them organized. For more details,

Execution role:

Execution role allows you to manage security on your operate, using described positions and guidelines or creating new ones. For more details,

Basic configurations:

Basic configurations allow you to determine the memory allowance and timeout restrict for your Lambda operate.

Network:

Network allows you to pick a VPC your function will access.

Debugging and mistake managing:

Debugging and mistake managing allows you to pick a Deceased Correspondence Lines source to evaluate unsuccessful operate invocation retries. It also allows you to allow active searching.

Concurrency:

Concurrency allows you to spend a specific restrict of contingency accomplishments permitted for this operate.

Auditing and conformity:

Auditing and conformity records operate invocations for functional and risk audit, government and conformity.

Lambda Functions

Accessing AWS Services

In your section, I will cover anxiousness of obtaining AWS solutions using AWS system, AWS CLI, and AWS Python SDK. The standard need is to have the AWS free account already designed.

AWS console:

With AWS system, all actions could be done using the web interface. This strategy becomes complicated working with many VMs. Also, we cannot have a programmatic design with this strategy.

AWS CLI:

AWS CLI for Ms windows or A Linux system can be downloadable from here. Using AWS CLI, all AWS solutions can be invoked using CLI.

Basic config steps:

After setting up client application, try "aws help" – If it works excellent, it means its set up excellent.

To allow programmatic accessibility aws solutions, accessibility key is required, go to security credentials-create accessibility key and obtain regionally and keep it safe.

AWS set up (specify accesskeyid, accesskey, area, outcome

format). For me, the area was Modifies name, but I had to specify us-west-2 which was the provisioning area. Possible outcome types are written text, JSON, desk. Desk structure is useful for simple studying, JSON is useful for programmatic circumstances where parsing is required for programs like python. "set up" option makes a config computer file in .aws listing with the above information.

Accessing Private Services or Resources

By default, your service or API must be accessible over the public internet for AWS Lambda to access it. However, you may have APIs or services that are not exposed this way. Typically, you create these resources inside Amazon Virtual Private Cloud (Amazon VPC) so that they cannot be accessed over the public Internet. These resources could be AWS service resources, such as Amazon Redshift data warehouses, Amazon ElastiCache clusters, or Amazon RDS instances. They could also be your own services running on your own EC2 instances. By default, resources within a VPC are not accessible from within a Lambda function.

AWS Lambda runs your function code securely within a VPC by default. However, to enable your Lambda function to access resources inside your private VPC, you must provide additional VPC-specific configuration information that includes VPC subnet IDs and security group IDs. AWS Lambda uses this information to set up elastic network interfaces (ENIs) that enable your function to connect securely to other resources within your private VPC.

Important

- AWS Lambda does not support connecting to resources within Dedicated Tenancy VPCs.
- Configuring a Lambda Function to Access Resources in

an Amazon VPC

- Configuring a Lambda Function to Access Resources in an Amazon VPC Typically, you create resources inside Amazon Virtual Private Cloud (Amazon VPC) so that they cannot be accessed over the public Internet. These resources could be AWS service resources, such as Amazon

- You add VPC information to your Lambda function configuration using the VpcConfig parameter, either at the time you create a Lambda function, or you can add it to the existing Lambda function configuration.

- The create-function CLI command specifies the --vpc-config parameter to provide VPC information at the time you create a Lambda function. Note that the --runtime parameter specifies python3.6. You can also use python2.7.

Internet Access for Lambda Functions

This section will talk about establishing AWS Lambda features to have accessibility to VPC sources as well as Amazon sources that are not straight connected to the VPC. This is a prevalent issue is you need to accessibility RDS or Elasticache example living within a VPC.

This details will talk about the few easy actions that are necessary to make Lambda features work with both VPC and Websites.

Amazon certification provides some rudimentary details to help you. The actions required are:

- Create a personal subnet within your VPC
- Create a NAT Gateway
- Create a Path desk with your NAT Gateway

- Assign the Path desk to your subnet
- Attach your Lambda features to the subnet

AWS Lambda Execution Model

When AWS Lambda carries out your Lambda function on your behalf, it requires care of provisioning and handling resources needed to run your Lambda function. When you create a Lambda operate, you specify configuration information, such as the amount of memory and highest possible efficiency time that you want to allow for your Lambda function. When a Lambda operate is invoked, AWS Lambda launches an Execution Context based on the settings settings you provide. Execution Perspective is a temporary playback atmosphere that initializes any exterior dependencies of your Lambda function code, such as data source connections or HTTP endpoints. This affords following invocations better efficiency because there is no need to "cold-start" or initialize those external dependencies, as explained below.

Note: The content of this section is for details only. AWS Lambda manages Execution Context creations and deletion, there is no AWS Lambda API for you to handle Execution Context.

It takes time to set up an Execution Perspective and do the necessary "bootstrapping," which contributes some latency each time the Lambda operate is invoked. You typically see this latency when a Lambda function is invoked for the first time or after it has been modified because AWS Lambda tries to recycling the Execution Context for following invocations of the Lambda operate.

After a Lambda function is implemented, AWS Lambda maintains the Performance Context for some time in expectation of another Lambda function invocation. In effect, the support freezes the Execution Context after a Lambda function finishes, and thaws the context as far as AWS Lambda gives the place when the LATBATE function is called as one. This external perspective shows that the following benefits:

- Any circumstances in your Lambda as they have remained, are still unwise and offer an interesting outcome when the case is called. For clarity, if your Lambda function works a difference only, instead of restoring the question, the unique relationship is used in the following eye. We have learned that it is a good thing to see if an association chooses to start it.
- Another perspective offers 500 MB of extra hard disk migration around the world. The large material corresponds to the following Temporary, continuous storage memory that can be used for different calls. You can add extra to determine if the information you have saved is.
- Background applications or callbacks created by your Lambda function that has not been established when the problem is solved, if AWS Lambda has chosen the Exodus perspective. You must ensure that all qualifications or callbacks (in the situation of Node.js) in your account may function consult.

Note: When your Lambda function is written, do not make AWS Lambda actually use the performance perspective for its future game. Other aspects may be required for AWS Lambda to build a new performance development, which can lead to unprecedented situations, such as between now and then. As often wonder, add reasoning to your Lambda functinn rule to opt for the only aspect of Performance Context.

Invoking Lambda Functions

Use the Invoke Lambda Function action to process Bamboo bedding notices, Jira work-flow changes, and Jira Support Table automated concept accomplishments with AWS Lambda, which lets you run concept without provisioning or handling servers:

You pay only for the estimated time you consume - there is no charge when your concept is not running. With Lambda, you can run concept for virtually any type of application or after sales service - all with zero management. Just publish your concept and Lambda manages everything required to run and range your concept with high accessibility. You can set up your concept to instantly induce from other AWS services or call it straight from any web or mobile app.

When building applications on AWS Lambda, including serverless applications, the primary components are Lambda functions and event sources. An event source is the AWS service or custom application that posts activities, and a Lambda function is the custom rule that processes the events. To illustrate, consider the following scenarios:

File handling:

Suppose you have a picture discussing application. Individuals use your application to upload photos, and the application stores these user photos in an Amazon S3 bucket. Then, your application creates a thumbnail edition of each user's images and displays them on the user's profile page. In this scenario, you may select to make a Lambda operate that creates a thumbnail automatically. Amazon S3 is one of the supported AWS event resources that can publish object-created events and invoke your

Lambda operate. Your Lambda Function read the picture

object from the S3 pail, create a thumbnail version, and then save it in the another S3 pail.

Information and statistics:

Suppose you are developing an analytics application and storing raw data in a DynamoDB desk. When you make, upgrade, or delete items in a table, DynamoDB streams can publish item update events to a stream associated with the table. In this case, the event data provides the product key, event name (such as insert, update, and delete), and other relevant information. You can write a Lambda function to generate customized statistics by aggregating raw data.

Sites:

Suppose you are making a website and you want to host the backend reasoning on Lambda. You can invoke your Lambda function over HTTP using Amazon API Entrance as the HTTP endpoint.

Now, your web client can invoke the API, and then API Gateway can path the request to Lambda.

Mobile programs:

Suppose you have a custom mobile application that produces events. You can create a Lambda operate to process events published by your custom program. For example, in this scenario, you can configure a Lambda function to process the clicks of the mouse within your custom mobile application. Each of these event sources uses a specific format for the event data. For more information. When a Lambda function is invoked, it receives the event as a parameter for the Lambda function.

AWS Lambda supports many AWS solutions as event sources. When you configure these event sources to trigger a Lambda function, the Lambda function is invoked instantly when activities happen. You define event source applying, which is how you identify what activities to monitor and which Lambda function to produce.

Moreover, to the supported AWS services, user applications can also produce events—you can make your own custom event sources. Customized event resources invoke a Lambda function using the AWS Lambda Invoke function. User applications, such as client, cellular, or web applications, can publish events and invoke Lambda functions on demand using the AWS SDKs or AWS Mobile SDKs, such as the AWS Mobile SDK for Android.

The following are introductory examples of occasion sources and how the end-to-end experience works.

Example 1: Amazon S3 Pushes Activities and Invokes a Lambda Function

Amazon S3 can publish events of different types, such as PUT, POST, COPY, and DELETE object events on a bucket. Using the bucket notice feature, you can set up an event source mapping that directs.

The following illustration shows the Amazon S3 to invoke a Lambda operate when a particular type of event happens.

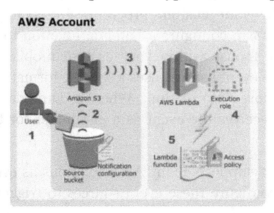

The following sequence is illustrated in the above diagram:

1. The customer creates an object in a bucket.
2. Amazon S3 detects the item designed occasion.
3. Amazon S3 creates your Lambda function using the authorizations provided by the execution role. For more information on execution roles. Amazon S3 knows which Lambda function to produce centered on the event source mapping that is stored in the bucket notification configuration.
4. AWS Lambda carries out the Lambda operate, specifying the event as a parameter.

Event Source Mapping

In AWS Lambda, Lambda features and event resources are the core elements in AWS Lambda. An event resource is an entity that posts activities, and a Lambda function is the custom code that processes the events. Supported event sources relate to those AWS services that can be preconfigured to perform with AWS Lambda. The settings is referred to as occasion resource applying, which maps an event source to a Lambda function. It allows automatic invocation of your Lambda operate when activities occur.

Each occasion resource mapping recognizes the kind of events to publish and the Lambda operate to produce when events happen. The specific Lambda operate then receives the occasion details as a parameter, your Lambda function code can then process the event.

Note: The following about the occasion sources. These occasion resources can be any of the following:

a) AWS solutions:

These are the supported AWS solutions that can be preconfigured to perform with AWS Lambda. You can group these solutions as frequent AWS services or stream-based solutions. Amazon Kinesis Data Streams and Amazon DynamoDB Sources are stream-based event sources, all others AWS solutions do not use stream-based event resources. Where you maintain the event resource applying and how the Lambda function is invoked depends on whether or not you're using a stream-based occasion resource.

    b) Custom applications:

You can have your custom applications post events and invoke a Lambda operate.

You may be wondering—where do I keep the event applying information? Do I keep it within the event source or within AWS Lambda? The following sections explain event source mapping for each of these event source groups. These sections also let you know that the Lambda function is invoked and how you manage permissions to allow invocation of your Lambda function.

Event Source Mapping for AWS Services

Except for the stream-based AWS services (Amazon Kinesis Information Resources and DynamoDB streams), other reinforced AWS solutions post events and can also invoke your Lambda operate (referred to as the push model). In the push model, note the following:

- Event source mappings are managed within the occasion source. Relevant API assistance in the event sources allows you to create and manage event source mappings. For example, Amazon S3 provides the bucket notice settings API. Using this API, you can set up an event source mapping that identifies the bucket activities to publish and the Lambda function to invoke.

- Because the event sources invoke your Lambda function, you need to grant the occasion source the necessary permissions using a resource-based policy (referred to as the Lambda operate policy).

The following example demonstrates how this model works.

Example – Amazon S3 Pushes Events and Invokes a Lambda Function

Suppose that you want your AWS Lambda function invoked for each item created bucket event. You add the necessary event source mapping in the bucket notice configuration.

The diagram demonstrates the flow:

1. The user creates an object in a bucket.
2. Amazon S3 detects the object designed occasion.
3. Amazon S3 creates your Lambda function according to the occasion source mapping described in the bucket notification configuration.
4. AWS Lambda verifies the authorizations plan attached to the Lambda function to make sure that Amazon S3 has the necessary authorizations
5. Once AWS Lambda confirms the attached permissions policy, it executes the Lambda function.

Note that the event is received as a parameter by your Lambda function.

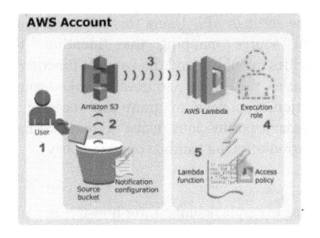

Event Source Mapping for AWS Stream-Based Services

The Amazon Kinesis Information Sources and DynamoDB streams are the stream-based services that you can preconfigure to use with AWS Lambda. After you do the necessary occasion source mapping, AWS Lambda polls the streams and invokes your Lambda function (referred to as the take model). In the pull model, note the following:

- The occasion resource mappings are managed within the AWS Lambda. AWS Lambda provides the appropriate APIs to create and manage occasion source mappings
- AWS Lambda needs your permission to study the flow and look records. You allow these permissions via the execution part, using the authorizations policy associated with the role that you specify when you create your Lambda operate. AWS Lambda does not need any authorizations to invoke your Lambda operate.

The following example demonstrates how this model works.

Example – AWS Lambda Pulls Events from a Kinesis Stream and Invokes a Lambda Function

The following plan reveals a custom application that writes information to a Kinesis stream and how AWS Lambda surveys the flow. When AWS Lambda detects a new history on the stream, it creates your Lambda function.

Suppose you have a custom application that writes records to a Kinesis stream. You want to invoke a Lambda function when new records are detected on the stream. You create a Lambda function and the necessary event source mapping in AWS Lambda.

The diagram below illustrates the following sequence:

1. The custom application writes records to a Kinesis stream.
2. AWS Lambda continuously polls the flow and invokes the Lambda function when the service detects new information on the stream. AWS Lambda knows which flow to study and which Lambda function to produce based on the event resource applying you make in AWS Lambda.
3. Supposing the attached permission plan, which allows AWS Lambda to poll the flow, is verified, AWS Lambda then carries out the Lambda function.

Event Source Mapping for Custom Applications

You can create a Lambda function event if you have a custom application that publishes and process events, no pre-configuration is required also you don't need to set up an event source mapping. The event source makes use of the AWS

Lambda Invoke API either. In case Lambda function and the application are owned by different AWS account, so in the permissions policy, the Lambda function must allow cross-account permissions associated with the Lambda function.

The following example illustrates how this works.

Example – Custom Application Publishes Events and Invokes a Lambda Function

The following diagram shows how a custom application in your account can make a Lambda operate. In this example, the custom program is using the same account credentials as the distinction that owns the Lambda function, and, therefore, does not need additional permissions to generate the operate.

Retry Behavior Is To Be Understand

A Lambda function can fail for any of the following reasons:

- The function periods out while trying to reach an endpoint.
- The function fails to successfully parse feedback data.
- The function encounters resource restrictions, such as out-of-memory mistakes or other timeouts.

If any of these failures occur, your function will throw different. How the exception is handled depends upon how the Lambda function was invoked:

Event resources that aren't stream-based:

Some of these event resources are set up to invoke a Lambda function synchronously and others invoke it asynchronously. Accordingly, exceptions are handled as follows:

Synchronous invocation:

The invoking program receives a 429 error and is accountable for retries. For a list of reinforced event resources and the invocation types they use, see Supported Event Sources. These event sources may have additional retries built into the integration.

If you invoked the Lambda function straight through AWS SDKs, the consumer gets the error and can choose to retry. queued before being used to invoke the Lambda function.

Get To Know Scaling Behavior

Concurrent executions refers to the number of executions of your function code that are happening at any given time. You can estimate the coincidental execution count, however, the concurrent execution count will differ depending on whether or not or not your Lambda function is processing events from a stream-based event source.

• Stream-based event sources for Lambda functions that process Kinesis or DynamoDB streams the variety of shards is the unit of concurrency. If your stream has a hundred active shards, there will be at most a hundred Lambda function invocations running at the same time. This is as a result of Lambda processes every shard's events in sequence.

• Event sources that aren't stream-based – If you produce a Lambda function to process events from event sources that aren't stream-based (for example, Lambda can process each event from other sources, like Amazon S3 or API Gateway), every printed event is a unit of work, in parallel, up to your account limits.

Building Lambda Functions

After uploading your application code in the form of one or more AWS Lambda functions to AWS Lambda, AWS Lambda will execute the code for you. AWS Lambda manages the servers to execute the code when it is called. The life cycle of an AWS Lambda-based application includes different sections.

Authoring code for your Lambda function in the languages supported by AWS Lambda. The supported languages are Node.js, Java, C #, Python and Go. These languages use specific tools for writing code. Some of them are AWS Lambda console, Eclipse IDE, etc.

If you implement code and create a Lambda function, you must first package your code and dependencies in an implementation package to develop a Lambda function. After you have done this, you must upload the deployment package to AWS Lambda, so that you can make Lambda function. Organizing your code and dependencies in specific ways is the first step towards setting up the implementation package. Instructions for the deployment package may vary, depending on the language you have chosen to write the code.

Uploading an implementation package is allowed by the CreateFunction operation of AWS Lambda, which is used to create a Lambda function. You can choose between AWS Lambda console, AWS CLI, and AWS SDKs to create a lambda function. Providing configuration data after setting the lambda function, including the computer requirements, is submitted to your implementation package.

Testing Lambda functions can be done by following one of the methods, such as testing your lambda function in the console or using the AWS CLI or even checking locally using the AWS SAM CLI.

The monitoring of lambda functions is automatic after your it is in production while reporting statistics are done via Amazon CloudWatch. This is the main problem of lambda functions. Take a look at our site for a better understanding of your lambda functions.

How Microservices Matured

The difference between microservices and SOA. SOA and microservices share a common pattern. Both are based on the concept of a service, and both ideally separate the interface exposed to a caller from the implementation. However, microservices applies a practice that is neither defined nor enforced by SOA. In essence, both represent the construct of an Application Programming Interface (API) within the context of a larger system.

The main difference is that a microservice employs a practice that attempts to eliminate any dependencies on other microservices. SOA does not make this practice explicit as a requirement; it's left as an implementation detail.

Suppose a developer builds a Web service that does a credit check based on a customer's social security number and some other basic information. In order for that particular service to function in an SOA-style implementation, it may invoke a chain of dependent services. With the microservices style, you would try and avoid forming those dependencies.

One of the things a developer should do when creating a microservices architecture is to set some finite rules. One rule should be that each particular part of the system, the discrete functionality, is autonomous, meaning that it functions all by itself. It has its own persistence, its own interface and its own wire-level protocols that it supports. The only way that one microservice should ever speak to another microservice is through a common network protocol, such as REST. SOA, by contrast, does not go so far as to dictate the implementation approach. In an SOA, it's left up to the system designer to decide whether those service chains should be called internally, in the processor through a network protocol. Here again, microservices is a more specific approach to building an SOA.

Services Loosely Coupled Microservices De-coupled Evolution of Microservices Is microservices, as some have argued, simply a way of "finally getting SOA right?" No, microservices is a subset of SOA and applies some additional rules. It is the adherence to those rules that gives microservices its own unique "mission" in application development and enterprise architecture.

Microservices As A Usage Pattern

It is commonly assumed the value of a microservices approach is that it represents a new architectural pattern and, therefore, leads to a superior application when compared with the monolithic approach. This is not necessarily true. The superiority of microservices is in its usage pattern or the style in which it allows programmers to work. Programmers prefer to work by doing something small, testing it, throwing it into a production environment, receiving feedback from hundreds of people, and making improvements. That is the cycle they favor, and microservices allows them to work that way. The same is true for SOA and Event-Driven Architecture (EDA) styles. In addition, programmers prefer to work independently, where they don't have as many dependencies on other team members. They are much agiler that way. They can build things faster, incorporating immediate feedback into work that might be only partially completed. This usage pattern is the greatest benefit of microservices—not necessarily what is achieved but how the microservices are used.

Decoupling large applications into smaller parts is a good idea; there are several styles of architecture that, in principle, offer the same advantage.

Imagine a developer deploys a microservice and someone tries to use it but realizes he can't because of some limitation. That person reaches out to the developer of the microservice and says, "I like what you built. However, I would like to use it in a slightly different way." The nice thing about microservices is that this immediate understanding of a limitation can turn into an immediate enhancement to alleviate that constraint. It is more of an Agile approach, as opposed to, "Hey, we're going to embark on a long project; we're going to design everything on paper, we're going to code it up and we sure hope it works and if you want it enhanced we will repeat this process."

Microservices And Applications

An application's construction has radically changed over the years as applications themselves have changed. First came the green-screen application, then the desktop application, and soon after the client/server application. Today, an application is a composition of orchestrated modular parts that are highly distributed throughout the enterprise architecture. Parts of an application exist in the SOA layer, the business rules server, the messaging provider, content management, storage tiers, caches in-memory and so on. The same application may have several different form factors. It may work on a tablet or smartphone as equally as it does on a Web browser. Applications might be process-enabled and drive business processes or interact with end-to-end processes. Trying to stuff all of this into one deployment unit, into a monolith, simply becomes "mission impossible" and does not lend itself for changing the application at the speed Digital Enterprises need today. The microservices architecture, therefore, is a welcome idea to help with the composition of a modern-day application.

Microservices in the cloud versus on-premises Is there a difference in how a microservices-based solution is deployed in the cloud versus on-premises? The short answer is no. In fact, the cloud offers a distinct advantage. One of the things about microservices architecture is that very little capacity planning is needed. It is possible to start small, relocate and replicates as needed. The benefit of running as a cloud deployment is the speed at which you can provision additional hardware, which essentially matches the speed you can provision microservices.

Therefore, expect to see modern applications that are built in microservices deployed more frequently in the cloud than on-premises.

The Serverless Logic Tier

We will use 2 AWS solutions for the reasoning tier; API entrance and Lambda:

API Gateway

Amazon API Gateway creates it simple for you to set up scalable and protected APIs. You determine techniques and sources just as you would in a REST API. Then you tell it which tracks need to perform what reasoning that you have described in Lambda features. Then it gives you https endpoints that you can tell your frontend rule to.

AWS Lambda

Lambda is my favorite part of technological innovation that has been created available recently. Basically, it indicates that you publish some features and with little settings, it can run and range as and when required as your representative. Lambda also motivates you to think of your programs as a decoupled set of microservices. There are no web servers to run (hence the phrase "serverless"), and you only pay for sources absorbed while the features run. You can perform an incredible number of demands for less than any money, and there are even a thousand telephone calls that you are given absolutely 100 % free every month which is awesome.

If you have ever handled web servers before, you know that it can be a discomfort to ensure your web servers are always protected or determining out how to autoscale and even how to set up programs at the range. Fortunately, if you use Lambda, you won't have to be concerned about that any longer.

You can produce a lambda operate run on various kinds of activities, like posting a computer file, operating on a plan or like in our situation, reaching https endpoints.

Configure Lambda functions

A Lambda function consists of the code and associated dependencies and also contains configuration data. You are the person who enters the configuration data when creating a Lambda function. API is also present so that you can update some of the configuration data. Lambda function configuration information is provided with the critical elements such as calculating the required resources, maximum execution time (timeout), IAM role (execution role) and handler name.

Calculating the required resources is done by specifying the amount of memory you want to allocate for your Lambda function. AWS Lambda allocates the CPU power to the memory in proportion to the same ratio as an Amazon EC2 general use device, such as an M3 type. In the example, it would mean that if you allocate 1024 MB of memory, your lambda function will receive twice the CPU share than if you have allocated 512 MB.

Maximum execution time (time-out) is specified to prevent the Lambda function from being performed non-stop. Because you pay for the AWS sources that are used to perform your Lambda function, this is pretty handy. After reaching the time-out, AWS Lambda ends the execution of your Lambda function. The recommended setting is valued at the expected execution time.

IAM role (performance role) is the role that AWS Lambda fulfills on your behalf when performing a lambda function.

The name of the handler is the method of the access point on which your lambda function code is executed, with eventual dependencies of event sources as part of your lambda function.

Amazon API Gateway

Amazon API Entrance is a fully managed service that allows designers to develop, post, maintain, monitor, and secure APIs at any scale. With a few clicks in the AWS Control Console, you can make an API that acts as a "front door" for applications to gain accessibility to information, business reasoning, or performance from your back-end services, such as workloads operating on Amazon Flexible Estimate Reasoning (Amazon EC2), code operating on AWS Lambda, or any web application.

Amazon API Entrance handles all the tasks involved in recognizing and processing up to millions of contingency API phone calls, including traffic management, permission and accessibility control, tracking, and API version management. Amazon API Entrance has no minimum fees or start-up costs. You pay only for the API phone calls you receive and the amount of information moved out.

Integration with AWS Lambda

If you want to build an API with Lambda integrations, you can use the Lambda proxy integration or the customized Lambda integration. Generally, you should use Lambda proxy integration for a flexible and streamlined API installation while providing versatile and powerful functions. The custom integration can be a value proposition if API Gateway needs to pre-process incoming request data before they reach the underlying Lambda function. However, it is a legacy technology. Setting up a custom Lambda integration is more important than setting up the Lambda proxy integration and the existing setup is probably not working when the Lambda function of the backend requires changes in the input or output.

Chapter Three: Benefit Of AWS Lambda

In this chapter, we will learn more about how AWS Lambda removes the complexity of dealing with cloud-based servers at all levels of the technology stack, its advantages and use cases and its pros and cons.

Business are benefiting by running their applications on the public cloud. There are several cost-saving advantages of using pay-as-you-go billing facilities. Organizations can improve their agility levels by subscribing to on-demand IT resources provided by cloud companies. Studies indicates businesses benefit directly by reducing their total cost of ownership (TCO) by migrating to cloud-based architectures. The total time-to-market also reduces considerably by moving to the cloud.

Even though the cloud makes it very simple to build and deploy the applications that run on them, companies can now avail additional benefits by using a cloud technology involving a different approach towards application design – One that can drastically reduce costs and offer much quicker time-to-market.

Cloud servers – Are they utilized properly?

cloud | server | Sunflower LabThe cloud eliminates the need for companies to own their own hardware and maintain expensive server-based architectures to run their business processes. However, a need remains to scale applications and maintain their reliability at the time of deployment. As business needs evolve and more processes are required to automate operations, companies have to scale up their cloud architecture by availing additional resources on their existing servers, or even order a new set of servers – virtual or physical – as and when required. Efforts have to be made to maintain good access times during peak hours and manage other activities when the traffic levels are low. From the operations point of view, there can be nothing more non-productive for a company than a server that remains idle most of the times. As per market findings, almost eighty-five percent of servers remains underutilized in a typical cloud setup.

Understanding Serverless Applications

There is then certainly the use of a serverless program, so what is it about conventional cloud stories? Multiple apps are designed in a more than what they can do on their core can be used, i.e., depending on the core quality that is there. The specific components of the app, such as the web and all underlying software, that handle the reliability and the correct application, are almost always derived from the developer. What remains is a clean, functional plan in which the business logic is activated only when necessary - in case a real poet presents a problem, an exception to the cloud if it is at a certain point and so on. An always best possible approach to make us stand out may have become important, and in place, the concept of running the code is only when something is done, even if it is introduced.

A serverless application running in the public cloud receives events and subsequently instantiates and executes the code. This model offers several advantages as compared to a conventional server-based application design:

No need to provision, deploy, update, monitor, or manage servers – All hardware and software is handled by cloud provider.

The application can scale automatically when. parallelization is fundamentally different compared to conventional applications which often require a receiver fleet and a special process to scale during peak load times.

In addition to scaling, all availability and fault tolerance aspects are embedded in the architecture. There's no need to code, configure, or manage the server to avail these capabilities.

There is no billing charge when the server remains idle.

AWS Lambda – The solution

AWS lambda | Sunflower Lab Lambda removes the quality of dealing with cloud-based servers at all levels of the technology stack and offers a pay-per-request billing model wherever you don't have to pay for idle computing time. AWS Lambda is offered as a computer service. It lets you run your code without provisioning or managing any different server. It executes the code only once required. It will scale mechanically to handle a few requests per day and even support more than thousands of requests per second. You have to pay solely for the server time you actually consume – there's no billing if your code is not being dead by the service. Moreover, you can run yours for nearly any type of application and/or backend services with zero administration costs. Lambda runs your code on a high-availability computer infrastructure.

It performs administration of all resources availed, as well as any server or in operation system maintenance activities, capability provisioning, automatic scaling, code monitoring and code logging.

You just has to supply your code in any of the supported languages – Node.js, Java, C#, and Python are supported now.

Lambda's Dual Economic Advantages

Lambda never remains "cold" since there is no "idle server time." Companies can benefit directly from reduced billing costs using the pay-as-you-go model. The service offers millisecond level billing granularity so no more rounding up of figures. If you've utilized a millisecond of Lambda than you just pay for that millisecond and not for the entire minute. This significantly reduces your cost of ownership.

Fleet management activities, including security patching, code deployment and monitoring of servers time-boxed redundant so you're not required to maintain associated tools and processes, and upkeep other tech activities to support 24×7 up times.

Lambda Applications Use Cases

Lambda's serverless application model is generic and can be applied to almost any type of application – From a startup venture's simple web application to a Fortune 100 company's stock trade-analysis platform. Here are a few examples where Lambda can be used:

- Web apps and websites

By eliminating servers, it is possible to design web apps that don't cost anything when there's no traffic. The server can scale dynamically at peak hours to handle excessive traffic loads.

- Mobile backends

Serverless mobile backends facilitate developers to easily create secure, available, and perfectly scaled backends without having to gain special expertise in designing robust apps.

- Media and log processing

A serverless approach offers natural parallelism so it becomes easier to process workloads. You don't need a complex multi-threaded system or require to scale entire compute fleets to handle heavy workloads.

- IT automation

Serverless functionality can be easily availed and customized as per need, as and when needed. It becomes very easy and simple to scale applications when the nature and scope of your business changes. If you're required to add or remove certain operational processes within your business model to adapt to changing market conditions, you can design and setup new modules without much hassles to automate your business the related IT processes.

- IoT backends

You can incorporate any code and native libraries to simplify the creation of cloud-based device-specific algorithms.

- Chatbots, voice-enabled assistants and other webhook based systems

A serverless approach can be a perfect fit for any webhook based system, including a chatbot tool. Since code is executed to perform certain actions only when needed, such as when an end user requests some information from a chatbot, AWS Lambda can be perfect choice for such applications as permanent threads are not required to keep communication channels open 24×7. The majority of Alexa Skills for Amazon Echo are implemented using AWS Lambda.

AWS Lambda is the most obvious solution. Before we reached, however, it was almost certain that we decided to use a cloud environment for the back-end of your application. With Lambda, Amnesty has developed a new development - Function-as-a-Service. In this case, we will make a short overview about AWS Lambda, and then use and disadvantages of the use of the most common.

AWS Lambda Overview

AWS Lambda is a SERVICE THAT WAS INSTALLED BY AMAZON WEB SERVICES IN 2014. It is about a separate unique environment for individual functions written in Node.js, Python, Java or C #.

Whereas a traditional web app need to server, which is constantly available implement In the course of web? N an EC2 or another hosting, for example, AWS Lambda removes the necessary for this by automating the provisioning and release of servers. Connected with a relatively new look, you have a little bit used to use AWS Lambda and you can use one of the many triggers to set up a good program. This allows you to call only when necessary, with a view to the last maintenance of the whole, regardless of the amazing AWS, in accordance with the industry standard, and with all reliability.

Pro: Shorter execution completed

One of the biggest functions of AWS Lambda functions is the most common of them all. In a great application, which is hosted on - and especially - by EC2 in AWS, you had to pay for the most common problems, from which your API is not actually used. This is a bit too much, but it depends on the particularities of the moment that you are working on it.

With the help of AWS Lambda function, you only pay for the computer user that you can use. AWS Lambda functions are widely used throughout the process of CPU time, which is considered a curse and a good price based on a similar moment. You do not have to scale your instance (for the most part - AWS does at least make you think of them of any change in the case), nor should you have a warning for a particular or web server. AWS handles all this for you.

If you are only active for yours, you only pay for one person - where you are largely deterred by whatever you want. In addition, the first (i.e., 1,000,000) requests per morning are from the other. If you think that you have ever received a different idea (with a number of transfer limits), you never have to pay anything!

Con: No continuous environment

To make this happen and ultimately to use it, you have to take control of your environment. While AWS Lambda works on Amazon Machine Municipalities (AMIs) and uses these tools for the web and the new developments, you are not able to use the real important software during the new adventure. If your code has all the necessary features of the operating system, it should be made possible - or hosted with almost every time!

Not at all, while AWS gives you useful tools to complete the process without errors, you are not sure that you will receive the same for each execution. In other cases, even if you are able to make use of the other way, all your choices could be processed in the next execution of your fun thing.

Finally, you will not only get more information about how it goes now. Many Lambda functions work in a warm, cold atmosphere, but also with ideas. The first thing that can happen to a finite after a bit of hard thinking instead is that if AWS represents a machine intended for your function - this is a "cold function." While this is true for about 10 seconds after you have chosen (making the right one "hôt-function," think that it is good without spin-up), after that the 10th your work will be subordinate

Pro: Improved Application Resiliency

Another benefit of AWS Lambda is that your code can now be a lot of resilient once under load and in sub-optimal execution conditions. AWS specifies that Lambda functions ought to be stateless, and with some careful architecting, you can additionally make each call idempotent. This frees you up to parcel out your application's activities to any number of handlers, each of which can use Lambda to execute your application's logic.

As your application is not hosted on a specific server, you furthermore may scale back your risk by not having to believe upon one machine to perform all the tasks of serving your app and executing your code – if one machine goes down, AWS handles swapping it out automatically, and your code doesn't miss a beat.

Con: a lot of Complex decision Patterns

While improved resiliency and reduced-price are important benefits, the style of AWS Lambda does have the potential to extend the design-time cost of your application. AWS Lambda functions are timeboxed, with a default timeout of three seconds (it is configurable up to 5 minutes). This means you wish to spend more time orchestrating and organizing your functions so that they'll add a distributed fashion on your data. If you have a process that is easily chunkable, such as video process, this isn't a problem, however other tasks involving large amounts of data can have a tendency to exceed the runtime limits, creating significant effort for your developers that now want to rewrite the code in a different design. A standard server-based application could handle this by launching another microservice, or by simply passing the object to the operative system to call a custom tool. These choices are not on the market in AWS Lambda.

Summary

Serverless application development is completely varied. For some use of places, often chosen is an important point, and it is lost for service marching is great time that can not be afforded. However, for more often web controls, often more often than that, you only had to say something that you can use in an "experience" that often occurs over time (with the definition of "really" that was created in that way).

AWS Lambda functions you to the flexibility leverage this lack of restriction, allowing you to your decouple application's code from your server architecture and create a more resilient, lower-cost application while sacrificing over some monitoring the implementation and execution environment length. Whether this approach makes sense for your decision is a good choice that you have to make to get to know your own - however much it may be and make sure that your decision is right.

AWS Lambda lets you work with provisioning or making games. You are only for the right time that you have yourself - there is no charge if you do not already walk.

With Lambda, you can execute the code for virtually any part of the trade-off or to start-all at zero. Just upload your code and Lambda will take everything into your code to enter and scales up with a lot of surprises. You can use your spyware to really find more of other AWS or to do it directly from any user or mobile user.

Chapter Four: Lambda Use Cases

Lambda Use Cases

The following sections detail some common Lambda use cases.

Web Services with API Gateway

With the release of AWS API Gateway, an elegant and scalable mechanism for making Lambda functions available as web services became available. Although initially somewhat lacking in features, the popularity of API Gateway in conjunction with Lambda has gone from strength to strength, and this isnow a common deployment pattern for lightweight and web-scale services alike. A tutorial later in this document describes how to build a simple web application that runs in Lambda fronted by API Gateway.

Batch Data Processing

Increasingly Lambda is being used for batch data processing. The cost model of paying only for required compute is compelling; for batch jobs or workloads that run hourly or more frequently, implementation on EC2 would result in 24/7-equivalent costs. For an hourly batch job that requires significant computation, clearly, this could be expensive. With the inbuilt ability to schedule the invocation of Lambda jobs, management overhead is further reduced.

Analytics

Following on from the above, but additionally incorporating streaming data processing, analytics workloads on Lambda are surging in popularity. Being a somewhat recent platform to be employed for analytics, frameworks and tooling are relatively immature when compared to traditional dedicated compute platforms, but the field is developing rapidly given the huge advantages of cost and scale. Dubbed "Serverless Map/Reduce," several reference architectures and open-source frameworks are available - PyWren5 is one such implementation, with which one benchmark achieved a peak of 40 TFLOPS, an impressive demonstration of scalable analytics compute capacity.

Event-Driven Processing

Throughout the AWS platform, events such as the arrival of objects in an S3 bucket or notifications from SNS can be used to trigger Lambda functions to process new data or otherwise react to the event. Consider the classic AWS example of an image upload site that needs to generate a thumbnail for each uploaded image - the S3 event generated by the arrival of each image Lambda Use Cases invokes a Lambda function with an IAM role that allows it to retrieve the image, generate a thumbnail and write the thumbnail image to the correct location in S3 from where it can be retrieved.

AWS Environment Automation

In the past, often one or more "automation" instances were employed in a typical AWS account to perform tasks such as EC2 instance out-of-hours shut down, EBS volume snapshots and other housekeeping tasks. With the facility to schedule Lambda function invocations now available, this means that maintaining a running instance (that needs to be managed, patched, etc.) is no longer a requirement. Given an appropriate IAM role, Lambda functions can perform all these tasks at a fraction of the cost.

Log Ingest and Analysis

As described above, logs from Lambda functions are streamed to CloudWatch, but ingest and post-processing to improve searchability and visibility are recommended. As well as this, logs from other sources often need on-the-fly processing. Lambda can be used as part of this pipeline for log traffic in flight - the ability to scale up instantaneously should the number of loglines/sec dramatically increase can be a lifesaver. During outages or incidents, when the volume of log traffic is often elevated, it's important to ensure the ingest platform is able to deal with the load, and it's also during these times that having a reliable logging platform is most important. Given the temporal nature of the data, and reliability of the platform, Lambda can be a good choice for these use cases.

Artifact Build and Test

A relatively recent, emerging use case for Lambda is within build systems - tests can be run with a huge degree of parallelization, without needing to manage and run multiple build slaves. Obviously, care must be taken that the 300-second invocation time limit is not exceeded, but with appropriate decomposition, this issue can be avoided.

AWS Step Functions

Introduced at Re: invent 2016, AWS Step Functions6 build on the underlying functionality of the Lambda platform and provides the user with a mechanism for coordinating and passing control between a number of small supporting Lambda services that jointly comprise a serverless application.

Lambda Advantages & Limitations

There are a number of reasons why using Lambda seems sensible.

A good part of our planned functions and services only run during areas of the day. There are always times of your efforts and effort where these circumstances sit nonproductive. And during those times you pay for your estimate sources. The payments interval on a Lambda operate is in the milliseconds, so it could considerably website.

Operating techniques and circumstances come with a functional expense. You need to handle these circumstances, spot them, observe them – all with a cost connected. With Lambda, you don't need to be worried about the actual circumstances because they are so temporary, and are re-provisioned each and whenever a operate operates.

On the contrary side, Lambda is not appropriate for all use cases; it does have its restrictions.

The program size and sources it can eat are restricted and not all programs are appropriate to run as Lambda features.

Processes that take a prolonged time interval of time to finish are also not appropriate to run as Lambda features. If you have a complicated operation that does 15 different things, it might be better to divide these up into several features or build a service out of them.

Chapter Five: Understanding The Basics Of Cloud Computing

In this section, we can introduce you to cloud computing and the key terms used normally by cloud experts. We seem to will briefly describe what public, personal, and hybrid clouds place device, followed by a summarize of various cloud service models (offered by the service providers), including the features of Infrastructure as a Service (IaaS), Platform as a Service (PaaS), and Software as a Support (SaaS).

To help you get started on Amazon.com Web Alternatives (AWS), we will end the chapter by walking you through the step-by-step process of creating an AWS concern and describing some of the salient features of the AWS sprint.

This area will cover the following points:

- Define cloud computing and describe some of its characteristics
- Describe and compare group, individual, and several clouds
- Explain and assess IaaS, PaaS, and SaaS thinking assistance delivery models
- Activities to create an AWS account
- A brief overview of the AWS management console

In 2006, Amazon Web Alternatives (AWS) began offering IT infrastructure services to businesses in the kind of web services—now commonly known as cloud handling. One of the key benefits of thinking computing is the opportunity to replace up-front capital infrastructure expenses with low different costs that scale with your business. With the cloud, businesses no longer need to plan for and procure servers and other IT features weeks or a couple of several weeks in advance. Instead, they can instantly spin up hundreds or thousands of servers in minutes and offer results faster.

Today, AWS provides an incredibly reliable, scalable, low-cost features platform in the thinking that capabilities hundreds of thousands of businesses in 190 countries around the world.

What Is Cloud Computing?

Reasoning processing represents the distribution of processing in form of something and not as a product. With a reverse phone lookup, application, distributed sources, and details are sent to devices like a utility over networks. This signifies that as an end user, you are not required to know the configurations and geographic place of the program used to deliver the solutions. This technological innovation improves abilities without the need for new facilities, workers and application certification. The solutions can be pay-per-use or registration centered. There are various benefits that customers get from cloud processing.

One of the main benefits of this processing is that it is easy to incorporate into other programs. The incorporation also requires a shorter quantity of comparison to others. You can incorporate cloud processing with both native and third-party programs. Users also get top quality solutions because the facilities provide more scalability. It is also possible to restore all your details after a tragedy when you are using cloud processing. The uptime offered by a reverse phone lookup is also impressive in comparison to other options.

This kind of processing does not require any installation of application or components and this creates it ones of the easiest forms of technological innovation. This signifies that capital expenses is lower when you use the support. It requires a very brief time frame to get the techniques launched and established therefore you do not have to wait for several weeks and invest a huge amount of money to get a new technological innovation solution. A few weeks or several weeks are adequate to get an activity operating even if it requires some personalization.

In to get the most out of any technological innovation solutions, it has to be personalized to get to know your particular needs. This technological innovation provides support for comprehensive personalization. This signifies that it can be used by huge businesses. One of the things that create a reverse phone lookup stand out is the fact that is can take care of the configurations that you set during the personalization procedure even after an update. This creates it a wise decision for organizations that are centered in an industry that is never standing still.

Cloud technological innovation improvements are automatic therefore they do not affect your IT sources. All the integrations and personalization that you carry out on your program will be managed during an update. You do not have to invest several hours and use a lot of sources to be able to update your program.

The phrase 'Cloud Computing' has already become one of the biggest IT buzzwords of the last few years. You may have seen the advertisements on the London Subterranean, heard your in-house IT team refer to it and may even have been asked to join in the cloud, but do you know what the term actually means? And are you aware of the functions it involves and how it may impact on your task methods and IT management?

In reality, there is no single worldwide definition for cloud processing as the term is really a catch-all or outdoor umbrella phrase. It is used to cover a great number of styles relevant on the internet perform procedures. It is most commonly used to explain the act of discussing details, data files and application over the web to customers in remote places.

Cloud processing when used to discuss important sources such as application programs and details are of particular significance to medium-sized organizations who, rather than purchase a new version of Microsoft Office or Adobe Adobe photoshop for example with each new hire, can simply provide access to the necessary resources via an internet-based, central area. Workers in any place can then login on the internet accessibility the program required to complete their task.

Cloud processing associates to IT freelancing in a plethora of possibilities, the most significant of which being that the business demanding accessibility for workers doesn't need to invest in buying, control and servicing of the devices required to host a great number of providers and programs. Outsourcing IT solutions in this manner have many benefits for small, huge and method enterprises;

- The ability to increase or reduce solutions on demand gives total versatility
- There are proven cost-saving benefits with the financial pressure of servicing removed and substituted for a set expenses
- Secure, global accessibility for all workers with a web-based accessibility
- Software and components demands in-house are raised, with the pressure of labor instead of being distributed across various network devices
- Reasoning processing and virtualization create maximum use of web servers, helping you perform towards an eco-friendly computer environment

If you have used an on the internet email support like Gmail or used Search engines Documents to discuss details with co-workers in other divisions or structures, you'll already have started to use cloud processing. The benefits of taking this concept further and moving out this performance across a range of programs, places and job positions, is what creates cloud processing such an interesting assumption for any enterprise looking to improve its perform procedures and IT performance.

Choosing a reliable cloud processing partner to manage organized solutions and keep web servers is of critical significance. Understanding the difference between other terms relevant to cloud processing including phrases like 'Software as a Service (SAAS)' and 'Platform as a Service (PAAS)' are important to the decision-making procedure. In other words, SAAS associates to a web-based solutions such as Search engines Mail that are utilized by directing to a particular place. PAAS allows for custom-built programs such as unique details research or confirming resources.

Six Advantages of Cloud Computing

Reasoning processing can bring you an IT facilitiy that is quick, responsive and has the ability to change the way you run your organization by removing current working challenges, allowing organization functions to operate a lot more resourcefully and providing you with option all the cloud technological innovation which is the most up-to-date you can get.

Most modern organizations know something about cloud processing these days, even if they haven't yet integrated it into their organizational structure. They understand it's a series of alternatives that allow them to use programs and share sources over the web. As alternatives improve and problems get smoothed out with encounter and time, the cloud is starting to attract house people as well as all kinds of companies.

The cloud has had such a big impact on the organization globe due to the removal of components, physical server area and purchasing programs to perform IT needs, and the long run is a positive one as alternatives dealing with implicit mistakes or other concerns continue to result in an improved support for customers. Protection is also a major selling feature for companies, now there are answers available to create the level of security and privacy of your cloud as effective as the standard dedicated server.

For any sized organization IT specifications can use up a lot of sources from acquiring the original application and components needed to managing the pc and network. It all takes in a lot of energy and time particularly if a problem occurs such as the pc accidents, gets a virus, or you generally notice a poor online relationship - never mind the costs involved overall, all of which can take away from the essential elements of running a successful organization.

Outsourcing IT to cloud processing providers creates economical sense particularly for those with no, or very small, IT divisions as prices for highly innovative technological innovation and application are cost-effective. There are plenty of providers to select from to ensure you will pick one that is known for being reliable - if it has a large client base then this can demonstrate if it is an excellent company to choose. Do a search around beforehand as there are many available, and ask questions - figure out how simple they are to use, if they have a excellent client support, and if they can provide what your organization needs.

The benefits of cloud processing for any business is big and as you grow, whether it is to combine with another organization, increase into other places or even another country, or produce a new line of products, innovative alternatives enable you to utilize your IT facilities wherever and whenever you need it. Consider IaaS, SaaS, catastrophe recovery or backup alternatives to help in the development of your organization and notice greater financial benefits. As you pay for what you use this indicates you can have the facilities you need for the peak times, without spending for it in the low times.

This specific aspect of cloud processing is linked with various essential benefits.

Lower Cost and Initial Investment

Cloud processing is much less expensive than getting similar alternatives in the standard way. Companies will be spending completely for the elements of the support that they require, which will in turn, affect the price.

The wind turbine is also going to be reduced. Company computers and a web-based relationship will be the only preliminary specifications. All other processing alternatives will be utilized later on, without challenging extra components.

Scalability

A cloud alternative is much simpler to range up or down than the standard processing support. This is the perfect option for organizations that require versatility.

Companies these days are trying to endure in a very competitive and intense organization environment. Many of them are forced to range down. Several other organizations handle to create it through, which calls for staff development.

The cloud can be seen as an 'elastic' medium. Each support can be customized and scaly to address individual choices and desires. Conventional processing alternatives will require the purchase of more components or reorientating in order to be customized.

Easy Management

The proven reality is that no component is linked with the availability and the production of cloud processing alternatives creates them simpler to handle.

An organization's IT professionals will be free of problems linked with available storage area or the manner in which web servers get applied. All concerns will be focused on performance. Apart from the proven reality that these alternatives are handled, they are also likely to increase efficiency.

In addition, an organization's IT professionals can be confident that all updates take place without their participation. Maintenance and improvements will be entirely reliant on the cloud support agency.

Taking It Anywhere

Cloud alternatives are 100 percent place separate. This can be an appealing factor for organizations that move frequently or for organization associates that have to do a lot of organization journey.

Cloud alternatives can be utilized from any place that has an online relationship. This indicates that essential tasks and organization functions will be available anywhere, anytime. Accessibility from any place permits works at house and office journey without too many arrangements.

It is also essential to mention that the alternatives are device-independent. They will be accessible on any laptop or laptop or computer, as long as it is linked with online.

Cloud processing has taken organization functions in a new era. Many people will be discovering the key benefits of this form of processing later on. It is not hard, flexible and affordable; just several benefits that should be mentioned.

Types of Cloud Computing

Reasoning processing has three different kinds of solutions to offer. Based upon on the users' requirements, each kind of cloud processing solutions employed either independently or in combination with others. Following is a brief on the three kinds of cloud processing solutions.

Software as something (SaathwS)

SaaS is also known as "on-demand software." The customers of SaaS instead of completely buying the certificate of different program rent the applying regularly and use them through a web internet browser. The variety of program made available by SaaS is very wide. There many programs provided by SaaS used by businesses that deal in cms, human resources control, bookkeeping, ERP, CRM and other relevant areas.

The software-as-a-service kind of cloud processing is growing very fast while the biggest market for software-as-a-service current is CRM.

Platform as a Support (PaaS)

(PaaS) provides processing systems to customers of cloud processing. It is also the link between the other two solutions provided by cloud processing, i.e., SaaS and IaaS.

A normal PC requires a processing system that contains components structure along with a structure of the program. Such a system is the base of cooperation of the applying and components that contains the device's os, structure and 'languages.' Hence, when it comes to cloud processing, in the

97

lack of a real pc, it is Platform as a Support that provides the customers with all that is required to write a processing system.

Some of the functions that PaaS offers consist of hosting, implementation, examining, and database integration and program style. Furthermore, cloud companies offering PaaS consist of a variety of functions to style, test, set up, host and run applications. All of these functions can be acquired by an individual as well as business clients by signing up to a single package with all of the functions included.

Infrastructure as a Support (IaaS)

IaaS is the third kind of processing via the cloud. Just like PaaS and SaaS deliver different program and components functions based on a cloud system, IaaS provides a virtualized system. The process of components virtualization shows customers only the subjective processing system instead of the physical functions. Such virtualization leads to enhancing what is known as 'virtual machine monitor' or 'hypervisor' that enables enhancing the third part of cloud processing, i.e., Customer interface as a Support.

Infrastructure that becomes available to the customers of Customer interface as a Support contains program, web servers, network equipment, and data-center space. The cost charged by cloud companies from customers generally depends on the quantity of activity done by the consumer and hence, is not fixed. There is, however, a minimum quantity of charge based on the variety of functions a person has signed up too.

The commitment of serverless computing

What if you could spend all your time and effort and effort building and implementing great programs, and none of your time and effort and effort handling servers? Serverless processing lets you do just that because the facilities you need to run and range your programs is handled for you. Focus your time and effort on your business. Divert resources from facilities management into searching for and providing programs to market quicker.

Examples of serverless applications

Web program architecture

Azure Features can power a single-page app. The app phone calls functions using the WebHook URL helps you to save customer information and chooses what information to display. Or, do simple custom remaking, such as changing ad focusing on by contacting a operate and passing it information.

IoT back again end

For example, Internet of Things (IoT) devices send information to Flow Statistics, which then phone calls a Pink operate to convert the concept. This operates procedures the information and helps to create a new upgrade in Pink Universe DB.

SaaS integration

Functions facilitate activates centered on activity in a Software as a service (SaaS)-based program. For example, save a file in OneDrive, which activates a operate that uses the Microsoft company Chart API to alter the worksheet, and helps to create additional maps and measured information.

Mobile back again end

A cellular back-end can be a set of HTTP APIs that are called from a cellular customer using the WebHook URL. For example, a cellular program can catch a picture, and then call a Pink operate to get an access symbol for posting to blob storage. A second operation is activated by the blob publish and resizes the picture to be mobile-friendly.

Summary

On this process, you can arrange and connect to your details from any computer that is linked with the World Wide Web. Your customer account does not are available on an individual PC or laptop computer but on the Web and your details are stored not using one hard-disk but, again, on the Web. This allows you to discuss all your details such as your films, images, records, etc. with whomever you want and that too immediately.

Interestingly, almost all of us are partly using reasoning processing in a way. All our details that are stored on the web servers of one or another company online such as Google or Picasa is actually a portion of a cloud-based processing program. This is why we are able to gain availability to the details stored in our e-mail options from anywhere we want.

Hence, the factors for details to be called portion of a cloud-based program include immediate availability, transferability flexibility. The best portion of it is that all the details that you own at different systems such as office, e-mail, cell phone and social networking sites will get synched. Do not be frightened, what is on the web does not actually have to be on show to the public. Just like your e-mails cannot be read by others, other details too will be secured and will be on the show to only those whom you plan to show it to.

One of the benefits of the reasoning is for business people. Whenever organizations buy computer systems, they have to buy several different certified application such as Microsoft company Microsoft Windows, Office and other area-specific programs. With the help of reasoning processing, professionals can get availability ready made computer systems that already have all the preferred application set up. The most important advantage to organizations in such a case is cost saving. Cloud processing solutions offer offers at relatively lower expenses because of several of reasons such as a large number of customers, low expenses and huge buys by individual organizations.

However, the issue of security continues to be a big question indicate especially for business customers whose details are of very delicate characteristics. There are three types of reasoning processing solutions -infrastructure-as-a-service (IaaS), platform-as-a-service (PaaS) and software-as-a-service (SaaS). The features that a customer of reasoning processing will be able to enjoy rely on the kind and solutions details he or she is using, i.e., PaaS, IaaS or SaaS. SaaS is the most widely used kind of reasoning website hosting service support.

Setting up your AWS account

1. Make your account
2. Go to the Amazon Web Solutions homepage.
3. Choose Indication Up.
   Note: If you've signed in to AWS recently, it might say Indication Into the Console.
4. Type the asked for username and passwords, and then select Proceed.
   Note: If Making a new AWS consideration isn't visible, first select Indication into a different consideration, and then select Make a new AWS consideration. When creating a new consideration, be sure that you get into your username and passwords correctly, especially your current e-mail deal with. If you get into your current e-mail deal with wrongly, you might not be able to access

your money or change your security password in the future.

5. Choose Individual or Professional.

   Note: These two consideration types are identical in performance.

6. Type the asked for a company or private details.

7. Read the AWS Customer Agreement, and then examine the box.

8. Choose Make Account and Proceed.

   Note: After you get a message to confirm that your money is created, you can login to your new consideration using the current e-mail deal with and security password you supplied. However, you must follow the initial procedure before you can use AWS services.

9. Add a transaction method

   On the Payment Information website, the kind the asked for details associated with your transaction technique. If the deal with for your transaction technique is the same as the deal with you offered for your money, select Protected Publish.

   Otherwise, select Use a new deal with, the kind the payments deal with for your transaction technique and then select Protected Publish.

10. Verify your cell phone number

On the Phone Confirmation website, kinda variety that you can use to accept inbound telephone calls.

11. Enter the code shown in the captcha.

12. When you're ready to get a phone contact, select Call me now. In a few moments, a robotic voice will contact you.

13. Type the offered PIN on your cell phone's keyboard.

After the procedure is done, select Proceed.

14. Choose an AWS Assistance plan

On the Select, an Assistance Strategy website, select one of the available Assistance programs. For a description of the available Assistance programs and their benefits, see AWS Assistance - Features.

After you select an Assistance plan, a verification website indicates that your money is being triggered. Accounts are usually triggered within a few minutes, but the procedure might take up to Twenty four time.

Note: You can login to your AWS consideration during now. The AWS homepage might keep displaying a button that shows "Complete Indication Up" for now, even if you've completed all the actions in the sign-up procedure.

15. When your money is fully triggered, you'll get a verification e-mail. After you get this e-mail, you have full accessibility to all AWS services.

16. Troubleshooting setbacks in consideration activation

Account initial can sometimes be late. Here are some things to double-check:

Finish the consideration initial procedure. If you unintentionally close the window for the sign-up procedure before you've added all the necessary details, your money will not stimulate. To complete the sign-up procedure, open https://aws-portal.amazon.com/gp/aws/developer/registration/index.html and login using the current e-mail deal with and security password you chose for the consideration.

Check the details associated with your transaction technique. You can examine the details associated with your transaction technique on the Payment Techniques website. If there are mistakes in the details associated with your transaction technique, your transaction technique might not confirm.

Contact your standard bank. AWS validates transaction methods by sending a permission demand in the form of a small cost. Banking institutions sometimes decline these read-write for various reasons. Speak to your transaction method's providing organization and ask that they accept permission demands from AWS.

Note: AWS cancels the permission demand as soon as it's approved by your standard bank. You are not charged for permission demands from AWS, but these cost demands might still appear on statements from your standard bank.

Check your e-mail for demands to find out more. Occasionally, AWS needs more details from you in order to stimulate your money. Look at the e-mail to see if AWS needs any more details from you to complete the initial procedure.

Try a different browser.

Contact AWS Assistance. If it's been Twenty four-time and you're still not sure why your money isn't triggered, get in touch with AWS Assistance for help. Be sure to mention any of the actions that you've already tried, so Assistance can more effectively repair the issue.

Note: Do not provide sensitive details, such as bank card numbers, in any letters with AWS.

The AWS Management Console

The AWS Control System is a browser-based GUI for Amazon.com Web Solutions (AWS).

Through the console, a person can handle their reasoning processing, reasoning space for storage and other sources operating on the Amazon.com Web Solutions facilities. The console connections with all the AWS sources, including:

- Elastic Estimate Cloud: a web-based support that allows businesses to run program applications in the AWS public reasoning.
- Amazon Simple Storage Service: a scalable, high-speed, low-cost, web-based reasoning space for storage support made for online back-up and preserving of data and program applications.
- Elastic Fill Balancing: a load-balancing support for AWS deployments.
- Amazon Relational Data source Service: a fully managed SQL database support.
- Auto Scaling: a reasoning processing support function that automatically adds or eliminates compute sources depending upon actual usage.
- AWS OpsWorks: a reasoning processing support from AWS that controls facilities implementation for reasoning directors.
- AWS Identity and Access Management: a directory support made for tracking system customers and providing ways of tracking information about how they get authenticated.
- CloudWatch: a component of AWS that provides tracking for AWS sources and the client applications operating on the Amazon.com facilities.

An AWS client can also handle his accounts, such as tracking monthly spending. A person can set up new applications and monitor existing ones. The AWS Control System also provides educational sources, such as magicians and workflows, to help customers adjust to the reasoning.

The AWS Control System allows each client to get and drop support links for a customized perspective. An AWS client can also perspective and team sources and applications that share common labels, and then use the Tag Manager function to quickly make a change across an entire resource team.

The AWS System cellular app allows a person to perform functional tasks from a cellular phone. The cellular app is obtainable from the Amazon.com Appstore, Google Play or the Apple App Store.

The AWS Control System supports Microsoft Edge, Firefox, Internet Traveler and Opera internet explorer. There are separate consoles for iOS and Android.

Using the AWS Serverless Application Model (AWS SAM)

The AWS Serverless Program Design (SAM) execution is now available under the Apache 2.0 certificate. AWS SAM expands AWS CloudFormation to provide a simple way of interpreting the time essential to your serverless application. The SAM execution is the rule that converts SAM layouts into AWS CloudFormation loads. Formerly, you could publish function demands to the SAM requirements and AWS would need to make corresponding updates to the SAM execution. Now, you can play a role additional features and improvements to all of SAM. You can hand the SAM database and recommend changes to the execution by making a take demand.

With SAM's actual execution being free, you can develop serverless programs quicker and further make simpler your growth and growth of serverless programs by interpreting new occasion sources, new resource types, and new factors within SAM. Furthermore, you can change SAM to incorporate it with other frameworks from the group for building serverless programs.

Chapter Six: Characteristics of Microservices

Microservices are currently the "in" thing in software development, and for a good reason. They help us build more loosely coupled, highly cohesive, modular systems that work well in a continuous deployment model. Deploying a small change to a single microservice is much less risky than deploying a huge monolithic application with several weeks or months' worth of effort.

This section has identified at least four main characteristics that all microservices should have: they have a single responsibility, share nothing, are monitored, and run as a cluster. In this chapter, we'll explore these in a little more depth.

Discuss Nothing

If you think about a well-developed category in an item focused design, it encapsulates a particular idea by interpreting community and personal information and techniques. Exterior consumers course only sees people techniques. Designers are able to muck around with the personal things as long as the agreement based on people associates is managed.

Consider microservices as really big sessions

They have a community API in the way of REST endpoints, idea lines, etc., as well as inner condition. Anything inside the microservice may be modified or modified, as long as those community agreements are managed.

This signifies that a microservice should take a "share nothing" viewpoint. Machine to execution as well as its information.

Private Implementation

As already described, a microservice's personal execution should be able to modify whenever you want. If a microservice is based upon on a distributed selection for its efficiency, that becomes more complicated to implement. I'm not discussing application collections with typical sequence adjustment features, selection assistance, and the like, but collections containing sector particular company reasoning.

Libraries that contain sector reasoning should not be distributed to other microservices and programs. Doing so causes it to be more complicated to upgrade the inner reasoning of a microservice without impacting other programs. Even if the selection is versioned properly, you still could end up in a condition where some programs are operating an obsolete way of the preferred company reasoning. Even if the reasoning is the same, there might be efficiency improvements that are made which don't get combined out to all the programs using that reasoning.

Again, if several programs have to modify at some point, that's usually a signal that the efficiency should be drawn into a habit.

Private Data

Not only should a microservice keep its execution personal, it should keep its information shop personally. How information is saved is an execution detail. It's not usually appropriate to people APIs it reveals.

In many companies, ours involved, the program has expanded up around only one, distributed databases. This seems sensible, as most program projects start out as a more monolithic program and develop from there. It can be expensive to set up a database and keep it, even if you're using a free database. As a result, all the efficiency tends to use this main database, if for no other reason than "because it's there."

However, as you move into a microservice globe, the sector limitations become better. Which assistance operates what information is now an essential point. With all the information in a database, it's very attractive just to be a part of to the desk that contains the information you need, rather than contacting to another microservice. But doing so just partners the two solutions in a way that may not have initially been developed.

In a perfect situation, a microservice should be able to exchange out its information shop, with none of its customers the smarter. Maybe a microservice is rather write-heavy, so shifting from a relational database to Cassandra seems sensible. As lengthy as people agreement is managed, it shouldn't matter. But if other solutions are based on those same databases platforms, it becomes more complicated to make that conversion.

Even if you're not modifying databases suppliers, making changes to the current schema (adding content, putting in order the desk connections, etc.) becomes more complicated and needs more synchronization between solutions if they share a databases desk.

Think about it this way: if you share your databases with other programs, that databases schema has now become part of people API for that assistance. Any changes to that information shop must be in reverse suitable with current customers.

Monitored

We began our trip towards microservices with only one or two microservices. As of this composing, we have close to 150 microservice circumstances operating being made. Tracking a number of microservices and how well they're doing is one thing, knowing the condition and wellness of 150+ is quite another. Blockbuster online, who has developed much of the work around microservices, is revealed to have 500+ microservices operating.

This signifies that your tracking techniques must develop. I once observed someone say, "If it isn't supervised, it doesn't are available." This is especially true with microservices. Without the right tracking, it would be very simple for a fed up microservice to go unseen in the audience of programs.

At HomeAdvisor, we make use of our assistance in finding the procedure, along with the Drop Wizard wellness check structure to observe the wellness of all our programs. Our techniques can find where microservices are operating, figure out if we have enough of them, ask about their wellness position and review problems to Nagios so that the appropriate on-call people are informed.

In inclusion, log gathering or amassing techniques like SumoLogic and Application Performance Monitoring (APM) program, such as AppDynamics, allows us to see the wellness of our solutions eventually, look for styles, outliers and dig into problems that appear.

Clustered

Even though microservices keep their information personal, they like to run in features. Having an anchorman of failing in your overall program isn't usually a wise decision. So, we rotate up several duplicates of our programs. If one example goes down, we have others to get the slack and provide visitors until our tracking program can aware someone and get the losing example re-booted. Multiple duplicates operating include that if there is a rise in visitors, we can add an extra example to back up the extra fill. We may even choose to duplicate information between the events so that they're not all dependent using one information shop.

The effects here is that microservices should be published with the supposition that more than one will be operating. If there's surgery that should only run once, such as a planned project, the associates of the microservice group will need to organize among themselves using something like Apache ZooKeeper.

This is simple to ignore during growth, where there's usually just the one example operating on the developer's laptop.

For example, assume your microservice operates an everyday review and e-mails the results to a submission list. In growth, this works excellent. The review is run and the e-mail is obtained. Analyze passed! Make to understand, we're done! But then the microservice strikes a setting (hopefully the test environment), and everyone gets three duplicates of the report! This is quite likely unless the microservice is created with the which there will be more than one operating.

Conclusion

Microservices are a great structural design when you're ready for it. In any structural design, there are some things that are essential to keep in mind. With microservices, it's no different. There is much to learn. While we're still studying ourselves, we've found some of the essential microservice features. Some adhere to well-known styles such as having only one liability and encapsulation. Others, while not new, are much more essential when working in the field of microservices, such as tracking and clustering of solutions.

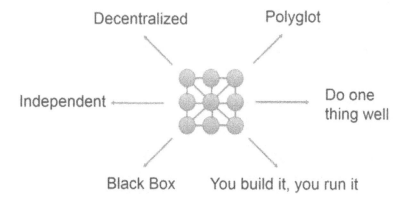

Figure 6.1 Characteristics of microservice

Challenges of Microservices

It is also clear that despite the advantages of modularization and containerization, many companies keep having trouble with microservices. In this section, therefore, I want to focus on what we've seen as some of the most common difficulties among companies and their common pain factors with microservices:

Challenges of reimagining and rearchitecting a program package product.

Probably the most important task for the applying designer considering microservices is the need to reimagine and re-think how the applying continues to perform. It is one thing to apply microservices in a Silicon-Valley start-up, and another for a business with complicated, heritage techniques.

Testing can become complicated.

Particularly with incorporation assessments, it becomes necessary for the quality guarantee professional to clearly

113

understand each of the different services in order to create quality situations successfully. Debugging meanwhile can mean the QA professional having to evaluate records across different microservice surroundings.

Effective control and group interaction required to avoid additional complexness.

While one of the main advantages of microservices are that in concept they should help technological companies reduced the complexness of working with monolithic programs, actually the reverse can take place as groups battle to organize their performance with so many different, quickly shifting components. This is why choosing efficient venture supervisors will be key to your ability to succeed.

Databases need to be absolutely decoupled from each other.

We have sometimes seen program designers discussing the same data source design across different microservices. This is something which shouldn't occur. When shifting to reasoning microservices, you need data source designs 100% decoupled from each other. However, it is also clear that despite the advantages of modularization and containerization, many companies keep having trouble with microservices. Therefore, I want to focus on what we've seen as some of the most common difficulties among companies and their common pain factors with microservices:

Challenges of reimagining and rearchitecting a program package product.

Probably the most important task for the applying designer considering microservices is the need to reimagine and re-think how the applying continues to perform. It is one thing to apply microservices in a Silicon-Valley start-up, and another for a business with complicated, heritage techniques.

Microservices And The Cloud

Microservices are separate programs that can be knit together into a larger program. Designers use microservices both to create new applications and as a design to break apart and refactor heritage monolithic applications for the reasoning era.

Getting Nimble with Microservices

Adopting a microservices structure can have many benefits, such as helping you to discharge program quicker, enhance your program more often, and even add new features more quickly. Organizationally, a microservices approach lets you devote more compact groups to more compact parts of the overall program. As these groups work individually, they can provide updates quicker. Microservices improve your team's ability to innovate, unblock creativeness and launch more often.

Why Systems Benefit Microservices

Using a database incorporation program to manage the health and lifecycle of microservices will boost the performance of your time and effort, as will an ongoing Integration tool, which takes liability for examining the rule, accepting it for launch, obtaining and posting it.

Using microservices does increase the number of unique programs that need to be handled, which possibly boosts the functional complexness of your environment. Systems create it simpler by managing much of that functional complexness as your representative. Your program will help you to range up your app when there's demand, watch for harmful instances, explain services speaking with each other, accept rule being offered by Ongoing Integration sewer-lines, and more.

Cloud Foundry Application Playback performs updates to the collections on which developers depend. Patching a collection becomes very easy across a navy of microservices. Platform providers can upgrade the control cell and main file system–the minimum level in a container–so that a moving upgrade of the whole program can be started off.

By far, the most common use of CFAR is for microservices. 54 % of those asked in our User Study use Cloud Foundry Application Playback for microservices, followed by websites (38 percent), internal business programs (31 percent), Software-as-a-Service (SaaS) (27 percent) and heritage program (eight percent).

What Are Microservices?

Microservices - also known as the microservice structure - is a structural style that components an program as an assortment of generally combined services, which apply company abilities. The microservice structure allows the ongoing delivery/deployment of huge, complicated programs. It also allows a company to develop its technological innovation collection.

Microservices are not a gold bullet

The microservice structure is not a gold topic. It has several disadvantages. Moreover, when using this structure, there are numerous issues that you must deal with. The microservice structure design terminology is an assortment of styles for implementing the microservice structure. It has two goals:

- The design terminology permits you to decide whether

microservices are a good fit for your program.

- The design terminology permits you to use the microservice structure efficiently.

The main concept behind microservices is that some types of programs become simpler to build and keep when they are damaged down into more compact, compostable items which perform together. Each element is consistently designed and independently managed, and the program is then simply the sum of its component elements. This is in comparison to a conventional, "monolithic" program which is all designed all in one piece.

Applications designed as a set of flip elements are simpler to understand, simpler to test, first and foremost simpler to keep over the life of the program. It allows companies to obtain much higher speed and be able to greatly improve the time it takes to get working developments to manufacturing. This strategy has proven too much better, especially for huge business programs which are created by groups of geographically and culturally different designers.

There are other benefits:

- Developer independence: Small groups operate running in similar and can iterate quicker than huge groups.
- Isolation and resilience: If an element passes away, you rotate up another while and the remaining of the program carries on to operate.
- Scalability: Smaller elements take up less sources and can be scaly to fulfill improving requirement for services of that element only.
- Lifecycle automation: Individual elements are simpler to fit into ongoing distribution sewer lines and complicated implementation circumstances not possible with monoliths.

- Relationship to the business: Microservice architectures are divided along company sector limitations, improving freedom and knowing across the company.

The common meaning of microservices generally is based upon each microservice offering an API endpoint, often but not always a stateless REST API which can be utilized over HTTP(S) just like a standard web page. This method for obtaining microservices make them easy for designers to eat as they only require sources and methods many designers are already acquainted with.

Is this a new concept?

The knowing of splitting programs into more compact parts is nothing new; there are other development paradigms which deal with this same concept, such as Service Focused Architecture (SOA). However, latest technological innovation developments combined with improving anticipations of incorporated "digital experiences" have given increase to a new type of growth sources and techniques used to fulfill the needs of modern company programs.

Microservices rely not just on the technological innovation being set up to assist this concept, but on a company having the lifestyle, know-how, and components in place for growth groups to be able to look at this design. Microservices are a part of a bigger change in IT divisions towards a DevOps lifestyle, in which growth and processes groups cooperate together to assist a program over its lifecycle, and go through intense or even ongoing launch pattern rather than a long pattern.

Why is free necessary for microservices?

When you design your programs from the floor up to be flip and compostable, it allows you to use drop-in elements in many places where in the past you may have required exclusive alternatives, either because of the certification of the ingredients, or specific specifications. Many program elements can be off-the-shelf free resources, and there are various free tasks that apply cross-cutting specifications of microservice architectures such as verification, support finding, signing and tracking, fill controlling, climbing, and several more.

A concentrate on microservices may also create it simpler for program designers to offer alternative connections to your programs. When everything is an API, emails between program elements become consistent. All an element has to do to create use of your program and information is to be able to verify and connect across those standard APIs. This allows both those within and, when appropriate, outside your company to simply create new ways to use your application's information and alternatives.

Where does package technological innovation come in?

The modern idea of light and portable OS storage space containers has been around since the early 2000s as an aspect of the FreeBSD venture. Docker offered an enhanced consumer experience for creating and discussing package pictures and as a result, saw great adopting starting in 2013. Containers are a natural fit for microservices, related to the desire for light and portable and nimble elements that can quickly be handled and dynamically changed. Compared with exclusive devices, storage space containers are meant to be pared down to the little practical items needed to run whatever the one thing the package is made to do, rather than packaging several features into the same exclusive or physical machine. The simplicity of growth that Docker and similar resources provide help create possible fast growth and examining of alternatives.

Of course, storage space containers are just something, and microservice structure is just an idea. It is entirely possible to create an program which could be described as following a microservices strategy without using storage space containers, just as it would be possible to create a much more conventional program within a package, which may appear sensible when you want to take advantage of package orchestration abilities without re-writing a large, monolithic app.

How do you set up microservices?

In order to actually run a program based on microservices, you need to be able to observe, handle, and range the different component areas. There are a number of different resources that might allow you to achieve this. For storage space containers, free resources like Kubernetes will probably take aspect in your solution. On the other hand, for non-container items of a program, other resources may be used for orchestrating components: for example, in an OpenStack reasoning you might use Heat for handling program elements.

Another option is to use a System as a Service (PaaS) device, which allows designers concentrate on composing rule by abstracting some of the actual orchestration technology and enabling them to simply choose off-the-shelf free elements for song of a program, like a data source storage space engine, a signing support, an ongoing incorporation server, web server, or other items of the challenge. Some PaaS systems like OpenShift straight use upstream tasks like Docker and Kubernetes for handling program elements, while others try to re-implement management resources themselves.

What about current applications?

While using microservices may be a significant element of a company's IT technique going forward, there are certainly many programs which don't fulfill this design, nor is it likely that those programs will be re-architected overnight to fulfill this new design. There is a social and technological cost of moving to a microservices structure, but luckily microservices and conventional programs can work together in the same surroundings, offered the company has a strong bi-modal IT technique.

Bi-modal IT, according to Gartner, is the capability to provide on both conventional IT programs with attention on balance and up-time, and more recent, more nimble but possibly less examined programs through more recent methods including things like the capability of designers to self-provision devices and short growth periods.

Serverless Microservices

It used to be that the big eat the little — nowadays the quicker defeats the slower. Quick groups keep their skills involved, deliver quicker, and defeat the competitors to market. Microservices let you enhance your technological innovation rate and rate.

Using microservices permitted SoundCloud to lessen a conventional launch pattern from 65 days all the way down to 16. The two blueprints below display before and after timeframes.

Length of set up pattern before microservices:

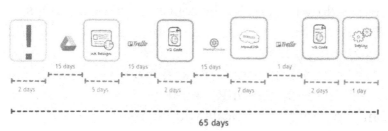

Length of set up pattern after microservices:

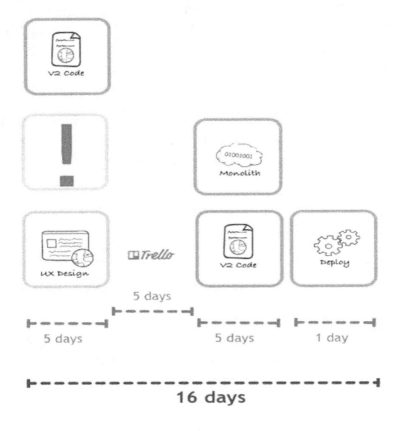

What is a scalable microservice?

- Services are little, provide an individual function
- Built on a scalable, serverless infrastructure: the support writer does not need to be concerned about DevOps
- Have continuous implementation and computerized examining (ideally)
- Are terminology agnostic: a knowledge researcher can create their design in R, and it can be incorporated into an app published in Scala with no issues

What is the extra edge of Serverless Microservices?

Focus on the rule, not servers

In monolithic programs, the designer has to keep the idea of the server because at all times. The actual of using an included microservice allows for various functions to be run in similar without impacting efficiency. So long as each microservice is published to be computationally effective, a designer doesn't need to concentrate on the web servers.

Write the rule once, use it anywhere

Imagine operating at a huge information company, and having the continuous issue of picture resizing across a multitude of web qualities. A resizing microservice would allow any professional in the org to add the resizing support to the rule they're focusing on with a simple API contact.

Language agnostic

Data Researchers often perform in Python or R, while system group may be in Scala or Coffee. Because microservices connect via API, it reveals up the opportunities for interoperability. Various open-source and cloud-based solutions are growing to improve the DevOps, popularly known as Be a Service or FaaS.

Composable

Microservices can be quickly used together, like components in a formula, to get the outcome you're looking for. For example, you could have one microservice that holds all of the images on your site, operates each through a experience identification microservice and a certificate dish identification microservice, delivers the images that contain encounters through a support that blurs out each experience, then delivers that picture back to your information resource to restore the uncensored picture.

Over time, your company will develop up a profile of preferred microservices that can quickly be found and consisting.

Cloud-agnostic

Microservices can give you the independence to use different blends of reasoning solutions. You may want to run your AI/ML designs on one provider's high-performance GPUs while using a different company for cost-efficient information resource internet hosting service.

Launch step-by-step features

Developers and groups can operate individually to create, set up, and range their microservices — they can also force repairs for insects without impacting the most of the facilities. This significantly makes easier the orchestration of timeframes by Item and Dev Supervisors.

Compliments other reasoning services

Modern programs make use of the extensive range of reasoning facilities that's on the market. Since these solutions are usually incorporated via APIs, microservices fit right in.

The financial aspects perform well

Serverless microservices are only unique up when required and all of the most important hosts only cost for what you use (often by the second or 100ms intervals). The benefits can be large — especially for AI/ML designs that often have great estimate needs that come in jolts.

Chapter Seven: Serverless Computing: Economic and Architectural Impact

Amazon Web Services revealed their 'Lambda' platform in late 2014. Since then, each of the significant cloud computing facilities providers has released services assisting a similar style of deployment and operation, where rather than deploying and running monolithic services, or devoted virtual machines, users are able to set up individual functions, and pay only for the time that their code is actually executing. These technologies are collected together under the promotion term 'serverless' and the suppliers recommend that they have the potential to significantly change how client/server applications are made, developed and operate.

This chapter provides two situations commercial research of beginning adopters, showing how migrating an application to the Lambda deployment architecture decreased internet hosting service costs – by between 66% and 95% – and talks about how further adoption of this pattern might influence typical application structure design methods.

'SERVERLESS' COMPUTING

'serverless' in the marketing terms refers to a new generation of platform-as-a-service offerings by major cloud providers. These new services were spearheaded by Amazon Web Services (AWS) but the system takes the role for getting and responding to client demands, task dispatching and arranging. Application developers are no longer in control of the 'server' procedure that listens to a TCP socket, hence the name 'serverless.'

ECONOMICS AND EFFECTS

Apart from the technical knowledge of the boilerplate code, most of AWS Lambda have an important effect on the systems that may or may not exist. Previous studies have shown the masters in the miraculous things - we know the effects during the startup of the plan. We discuss how it is possible that, regardless of architectural decisions, we have looked closely when we are sure that everything is going well.

With all the confidence in the chaos of the ominous way of hosting, the most worrying decision is a major concern. Failover and loading are very important because they only have the capacity of a single one. Codes assume that they have faith all over the world or override their stand-by sessions that they can take over if the primary result fails first. Each service will thus contribute to proportionality, with the associated capacity and planning for disaster recovery. With AWS Lambda, where probably only the first process will follow, there is only an attack when an application is active, other than when it applies.

With AWS Lambda, it would only be possible for 200 mids of every five seconds. Tisble 1 is a good idea of how such a decision should be made at various locations, whether or not existing. The smallest company chosen on AWS EC2, with an estimated total value of 512 MB, takes about 0.0059 hours per hour. Running two random machines (from and to the outside) would cost $ 0.0118. For comparison: a 512MB Lambda, which costs about 100 million dollars, costs 0.000000834 USD, so if you do it 200 ms per minute, you would definitely need $ 0,000020016, a cost-saving measure of more than 99, 8%. EC2 is not only important, but Lambda also does that, so if the demand costs less, it might be even more fun. With a 128MB

Lambda, it should probably be $ 0.000004992, resulting in a cost of more than 99.95%. Note that with Lambda there is no need to reserve a number of fail-over authorities, as the platform actually intends.

Another current trend aims that at improving utilization of reserved instances containerization is using technologies such as Lambda that was first announced at the end 2014, and which saw significant adoption in mid to end of 2016. All major cloud service providers now offer similar services as Google Cloud Functiisni, Azure Functions and. This is really strange AWS Lambda because this was the first place to play and is the most completely happy.

But, developers of applications would enrich themselves with all those special machines, usually hosted in what they needed, to other systems. The eye-catching expenses needed to come up with new applications and what is still going on was bad. Sweet times to see that the capacity was long, and dealing with the story can be explained in different with different, pre-planned planning, and often very interesting (and affordable) for many machines that had remained ignorant, rather than always considered.

This is an important consist of the application internet hosting service platform-as-a service generation of providers. Rather than continuously-running web servers, we set up 'functions' that operate as event handlers and only pay for CPU time when strikes are executing. Traditional client/server architectures involve a server procedure, typically listening to a TCP socket, waiting for customers to connect and send requests. A well-used example of this is the popular web server or a message line audience.

Conclusion

AWS Lambda lets you run code without provisioning or managing servers 24/7. You pay only for the compute time you consume—there is no charge when your code is not running. With Lambda, you can run code for virtually any type of application or backend service—all with zero administration. Just upload your code, and Lambda takes care of everything required to run and scale your code with high availability. You can set up your code to automatically trigger from other AWS services, or you can call it directly from any web or mobile app.

AWS provides building blocks that you can assemble quickly to support virtually any workload. With AWS, you'll find a complete set of highly available services that are designed to work together to build sophisticated scalable applications.

You have access to highly durable storage, low-cost computer, high-performance databases, management tools, and more. All this is available without up-front cost, and you pay for only what you use. These services help organizations move faster, lower IT costs, and scale. AWS is trusted by the largest enterprises and the hottest start-ups to power a wide variety of workloads, including web and mobile applications, game development, data processing and warehousing, storage, archive, and any others.

AWS offers a large portfolio of managed services that help product teams build microservices architectures and minimize architectural and operational complexity. This book guides you through the relevant AWS services and how to implement typical patterns such as service discovery or event sourcing natively with AWS services.

Since a couple of several weeks before its launch, Amazon.com has been marketing their new AWS industry to no end. Is it as excellent as the organization is saying or is it just another ordinary program? Amazon.com AWS industry was set up with the purpose of putting all of the Amazon.com Device Pictures spot. The information involved with each AMI is costs, opinions, and all of this in a simple, user-friendly user interface.

What 'serverless' really indicates is that as a designer, you don't have to think about those web servers. You just concentrate on the rule.

The Serverless Movement

Serverless has become an activity about designer power. As a technological innovation, it abstracts away the most basic areas of building a software, making you free to actually spend your days programming.

What this implies is that you, the designer, can quickly develop applications that manage production-ready visitors. You don't have to definitely manage climbing for your programs. You don't have to supply web servers or pay for sources that go rarely used.

The technologies are still beginning, but countless numbers of designers are already showing that serverless can allow them to discharge programs at history rate and price.

What makes a software serverless?

The serverless activity began with the discharge of AWS Lambda, a Function-as-a-Service (FaaS) estimate support. But serverless is much more than just FaaS.

Ultimately, serverless is about concentrating your time and effort on what provides value to your customers. This indicates using handled solutions for the data source, search indices, lines, SMS texting, and email distribution. It indicates attaching these types of solutions together using stateless, ephemeral estimate like the various FaaS promotions.

Upgrading your Linux system distro does not offer value to your customers. Handling your RabbitMQ web servers do not offer value to your customers. The delivery product provides value to your customers.

Focus on your company reasoning, not your web servers.

Benefits of Serverless Applications

These are the 4 primary advantages of Serverless Applications you should know about:

Zero management:

Set up rule without provisioning anything beforehand, or managing anything subsequently. There is no idea of a navy, an example, or even an os. No more disturbing the Ops division.

Auto-scaling:

Let your companies manage the climbing difficulties. No need to fireside signals or create programs to range up and down. Handle quick jolts of visitors and end of the week lulls the same way -- with fulfillment.

Pay-per-use:

Function-as-a-service estimate and handled solutions billed centered on utilization rather than pre-provisioned potential. You can have complete source utilization without a penny for nonproductive time. The results? 90% cost-savings over a reasoning VM, and the fulfillment of understanding that you never pay for sources you don't use.

Increased speed:

Reduce the cycle between having an idea and implementing to manufacturing. Because there's less to supply in advance and less to deal with after implementation, more compact groups can deliver more functions. It's easier than ever to make your idea live.

The Serverless Framework

If the Serverless Program is the new and enhanced application home on the prevention, then the Serverless Structure is the doorway you use to get into that home.

Serverless Applications are the next step in cloud-native growth, and they require automated. If you're attaching together several handled solutions and functions, you cannot depend on guidelines of guide actions. You should be able to reproduce your whole application with an order.

That is where the Serverless Structure comes in. Use the Serverless Structure CLI to develop and deploy you to any and every reasoning company with a regular experience. The Structure instantly configures reasoning source configurations for you, centered on which you use and the reasoning company you deploy to.

Keeping a maniacal concentrate on company value is applicable to your growth pedaling as well. Children, don't move your own implementation resources.

Benefits of the Serverless Framework:

These are the 4 primary advantages of the Serverless Structure you should know about:

Increase growth rate:

The Serverless Structure CLI allows designers to develop,

analyze, and deploy all in the same atmosphere. Developers create their functions in cloud-agnostic Serverless YAML, and solutions can be implemented with a individual control. Transactionally deploy rule to several suppliers, edition your deployments, and move back the implementation if necessary.

Avoid source lock-in:

Different reasoning suppliers all have different required types and implementation techniques. The Structure puts together you into an individual program that can be implemented across any reasoning company, abstracting away any necessary remodeling.

Infrastructure as Code:

Set up facilities across several atmospheres. Serverless easily combines with every Serverless Compute Service so that you can formalize and standardize your whole facilities as rule.

Existing atmosphere:

The Serverless Structure is pluggable, and many a multitude of community-contributed plug-ins are available in our GitHub Plugins repo. The Serverless Structure is commonly implemented, significance there are always effective conversations on boards and there are a variety of guides that will help you begin.

Amazon AWS Marketplace Positives

Amazon has made it a lot more readily discovered their AMIs by requirements. The industry is simple to search and once you are a participant, you can easily begin instantly. The payments process is clear and understandable and clients pay through Amazon.com as they would with any other support offered by the organization.

While the idea is excellent, it is not an industry like you would think, at least not yet. However, up to now, Amazon.com is the only organization that has come out with this type of industry.

Business entrepreneurs who are looking to flourish to the reasoning, and increase their existence in the reasoning can definitely take advantage of the new on the internet industry. It allows for preconfigured configurations in purchasing trolleys and allows them to add more technological solutions.

Small entrepreneurs will now be able to provide solutions as well as from significant organizations like 10gen and Microsoft company.

Amazon AWS Marketplace Isn't That Impressive

It could be the fact that it is a new user interface, and it may be because they have not involved everything they wished to add yet. However, the industry really isn't all that amazing. The exclusive equipment is not anything we have not seen before and there isn't much room for custom configurations.

While it isn't very amazing yet, Amazon.com could have some excitement in shop for us when they start getting customer opinions and see opinions of their product on the internet. Genuinely, releasing any system that contains an on the internet industry is a big step for Amazon.com. After all, we have not seen anything like it from their opponents.

The Biggest Benefit

Throughout all of the rumors of what everyone believes may occur with the Amazon.com AWS industry, there are a lot of advantages that can be seen. Like any new system that becomes available, it begins off little and produces through customer opinions and the needs of clients.

The best take advantage of the new industry is that it can easily be with the payments you already get from Amazon.com solutions. This makes monitoring costs a lot simpler for a little organization. The support also has the possibility to help organizations become bigger, more self-sufficient organizations in the long run. It allows them to work with significant organizations and get their practical more recent items a lot simpler than they could have before.

What Products Can Be In the marketplace

The items that can be seen in the Amazon.com AWS Marketplace is free, professional application, and technology application.